ACCOUNTS PREPARATION II

Qualifications and Credit Framework

Level 3 Diploma in Accounting

British Library Cataloguing-in-Publication Data

A catalogue record for this book is available from the British Library.

Published by
Kaplan Publishing UK
Unit 2, The Business Centre
Molly Millars Lane
Wokingham
Berkshire
RG41 2QZ

ISBN 978-0-85732-367-5

The text in this material and any others made available by any Kaplan Group company does not amount to advice on a particular matter and should not be taken as such. No reliance should be placed on the content as the basis for any investment or other decision or in connection with any advice given to third parties. Please consult your appropriate professional adviser as necessary. Kaplan Publishing Limited and all other Kaplan group companies expressly disclaim all liability to any person in respect of any losses or other claims, whether direct, indirect, incidental, consequential or otherwise arising in relation to the use of such materials.

Printed and bound in Great Britain.

We are grateful to the Association of Accounting Technicians for permission to reproduce past assessment materials and example tasks based on the new syllabus. The solutions to past answers and similar activities in the style of the new syllabus have been prepared by Kaplan Publishing.

CONTENTS

STUDY TEXT AND WORKBOOK

INTRODUCTION

HOW TO USE THESE MATERIALS

These Kaplan Publishing learning materials have been carefully designed to make your learning experience as easy as possible and to give you the best chance of success in your AAT assessments.

They contain a number of features to help you in the study process.

The sections on the Unit Guide, the Assessment and Study Skills should be read before you commence your studies.

They are designed to familiarise you with the nature and content of the assessment and to give you tips on how best to approach your studies.

STUDY TEXT

This study text has been specially prepared for the revised AAT qualification introduced in July 2010.

It is written in a practical and interactive style:

- key terms and concepts are clearly defined

- all topics are illustrated with practical examples with clearly worked solutions based on sample tasks provided by the AAT in the new examining style

- frequent activities throughout the chapters ensure that what you have learnt is regularly reinforced

- 'pitfalls' and 'examination tips' help you avoid commonly made mistakes and help you focus on what is required to perform well in your examination

- practice workbook activities can be completed at the end of each chapter.

WORKBOOK

The workbook comprises:

Practice activities at the end of each chapter with solutions at the end of the text, to reinforce the work covered in each chapter.

The questions are divided into their relevant chapters and students may either attempt these questions as they work through the textbook, or leave some or all of these until they have completed the textbook as a final revision of what they have studied.

ICONS

The study chapters include the following icons throughout.

They are designed to assist you in your studies by identifying key definitions and the points at which you can test yourself on the knowledge gained.

 Definition

These sections explain important areas of Knowledge which must be understood and reproduced in an assessment

 Example

The illustrative examples can be used to help develop an understanding of topics before attempting the activity exercises

 Activity

These are exercises which give the opportunity to assess your understanding of all the assessment areas.

UNIT GUIDE

Accounts preparation II is divided into three units but for the purposes of assessment these units will be combined.

Prepare final accounts for sole traders (Skills)

4 credits

Prepare accounts for partnerships (Knowledge and skills)

2 credits

Principles of accounts preparation (Knowledge)

1 credit

Purpose of the units

The AAT has stated that the general purpose of these units is designed to develop basic double entry skills and knowledge, such as that acquired in the level 2 units Basic Accounting I and Basic Accounting II.

The logical progression from Accounts Preparation I is to Accounts Preparation II, which deals with final accounts, but the sequence in which the units are taken is not mandatory, although it is recommended to complete Accounts Preparation I before Accounts Preparation II.

The unit is concerned with preparing final accounts for sole traders and partnerships, incorporating elements of dealing with incomplete records, and an appropriate understanding of the principles that underpin the preparation of final accounts.

After completion of both Accounts Preparation units, the learner will be ready to start developing skills and knowledge for the level 4 unit, Financial Statements.

Learning objectives

On completion of these units the learner will be able to:

- Prepare final accounts for sole traders
- Prepare accounts for partnerships
- Understand the principles of accounts preparation

Learning outcomes and assessment criteria

The unit consists of eight learning outcomes, three for Knowledge and five for Skills, which are further broken down into Assessment criteria. These are set out in the following table with Learning Outcomes in bold type and Assessment criteria listed underneath each Learning Outcome. Reference is also made to the relevant chapter within the text.

Knowledge and Skills – Prepare accounts for partnerships

To perform this unit effectively you will need to know and understand the following:

	Chapter

1   Have a basic understanding of legislation relating to the formation of a partnership

1.1	Describe the key components of a partnership agreement	2
1.2	Identify and describe the key components of partnership accounts	2

- Profit and loss account (income statement)
- Partnership appropriation account
- Goodwill
- Partners' current accounts
- Partners' capital accounts
- Balance sheet (statement of financial position)

2   Prepare a profit and loss appropriation account

2.1	Prepare the profit and loss (income statement) appropriation account for a partnership	2
2.2	Accurately determine the allocation of profit to partners after allowing for interest on capital, interest on drawings and any salary paid to partner(s)	2
2.3	Prepare the current accounts for each partner and calculate the closing balance	2

3   Prepare a balance sheet relating to a partnership

3.1	Record accurately the closing balances on each partner's capital and current accounts, including drawings.	2
3.2	Prepare a balance sheet (statement of financial position) for a partnership, in compliance with the partnership agreement.	2

Skills – Prepare final accounts for sole traders

To perform this unit effectively you will need to be able to do the following.

Chapter

1   Prepare accounting records from incomplete information

1.1	Calculate accurately the opening and/or closing capital using incomplete information	3
1.2	Calculate accurately the opening and/or closing cash/bank account balance	3
1.3	Prepare sales and purchase ledger control accounts and use these to correctly calculate sales, purchases and bank figures	3
1.4	Prepare accurately journal entries or ledger accounts to take account of	1,3

- Closing stock
- Accruals and prepayments
- Depreciation
- Allowance for doubtful debts
- The gain/loss on disposal of a fixed asset
- Purchase of assets

2   Produce accurate final accounts

2.1	Produce a trial balance from accounting information	1,3
2.2	Prepare a profit and loss account (income statement)	1,3
2.3	Prepare a balance sheet (statement of financial position)	1,3

KAPLAN PUBLISHING

Delivery guidance

The AAT have provided delivery guidance giving further details of the way in which the unit will be assessed.

Students should be familiar with interchangeable terminology including IAS and UK GAAP.

Prepare final accounts for sole traders

The learner will be expected to prepare accounting records from incomplete information.

The learner will be able to calculate opening and closing cash/bank balances. Establish sales, purchases and bank figures by using control accounts.

They will be able to calculate accurately opening and/or closing capital.

The learner should be able to construct 'T' accounts to establish the missing figures and also be able to account balances with the use of mark ups and margins.

The learners should be able to prepare a profit and loss account (income statement), for which a skeleton pro forma will be given; from a given full balancing adjusted trial balance which may include balances on accounts such as fixed asset disposals, depreciation charges and other adjustments that are dealt with in Accounts Preparation I.

A skeleton pro forma will also be given to complete a balance sheet (statement of financial position) from a given trial balance as for the profit and loss account.

Prepare accounts for partnerships

The learner will be expected to prepare a profit and loss appropriation account and a balance sheet relating to a partnership.

The number of partners in the question will be limited to a maximum of three and learners will be expected to deal with a maximum of one change during the period.

Goodwill must be dealt with correctly by introducing goodwill and then eliminating it from the accounting records.

The learner will be given a balancing trial balance and an outline balance sheet to complete. The learners are also expected to prepare the current accounts for each partner which may include interest on capital, interest on drawings, drawings, salary and profit share.

Principles of accounts preparation

The learner will also need to demonstrate an appropriate understanding of the principles that lie behind these accounting procedures, including an awareness of the accounting systems that must be in place in order to produce meaningful information at the end of an accounting period.

The learner should also develop an understanding of the environment and principles within which the business operates.

KAPLAN PUBLISHING

THE ASSESSMENT

The format of the assessment

The assessment will be divided into two sections.

Section 1 covers:

This section is about incomplete records and will comprise of two independent tasks.

A variety of techniques for finding missing figures will be required, including a selection from:

- Using the accounting equation
- Using mark – up or margin
- Reconstructing the capital account
- Reconstructing the bank account
- Reconstructing control accounts – purchases, sales, VAT

Section 2 covers:

This section is about final accounts for sole traders and partnerships and will comprise four independent tasks which will include:

- Preparing a profit and loss account from a final trial balance
- Preparing ledger accounts or making calculations to deal with partnership accounts such as admission or retirement of a partner
- Preparing a partnership appropriation account or current accounts
- Preparing a balance sheet from a final trial balance
- Short answer questions to test the knowledge parts of the relevant units.

Learners will normally be assessed by computer based assessment (CBA), and will be required to demonstrate competence in both sections of the assessment.

Time allowed

The time allowed for this assessment is **two hours**.

STUDY SKILLS

Preparing to study

Devise a study plan

Determine which times of the week you will study.

Split these times into sessions of at least one hour for study of new material. Any shorter periods could be used for revision or practice.

Put the times you plan to study onto a study plan for the weeks from now until the assessment and set yourself targets for each period of study – in your sessions make sure you cover the whole course, activities and the associated questions in the workbook at the back of the manual.

If you are studying more than one unit at a time, try to vary your subjects as this can help to keep you interested and see subjects as part of wider knowledge.

When working through your course, compare your progress with your plan and, if necessary, re-plan your work (perhaps including extra sessions) or, if you are ahead, do some extra revision / practice questions.

Effective studying

Active reading

You are not expected to learn the text by rote, rather, you must understand what you are reading and be able to use it to pass the assessment and develop good practice.

A good technique is to use SQ3Rs – Survey, Question, Read, Recall, Review:

1   Survey the chapter

Look at the headings and read the introduction, knowledge, skills and content, so as to get an overview of what the chapter deals with.

2   Question

Whilst undertaking the survey ask yourself the questions you hope the chapter will answer for you.

3   Read

Read through the chapter thoroughly working through the activities and, at the end, making sure that you can meet the learning objectives highlighted on the first page.

4   Recall

At the end of each section and at the end of the chapter, try to recall the main ideas of the section / chapter without referring to the text. This is best done after short break of a couple of minutes after the reading stage.

5   Review

Check that your recall notes are correct.

You may also find it helpful to re-read the chapter to try and see the topic(s) it deals with as a whole.

Note taking

Taking notes is a useful way of learning, but do not simply copy out the text.

The notes must:

- be in your own words
- be concise
- cover the key points
- well organised
- be modified as you study further chapters in this text or in related ones.

Trying to summarise a chapter without referring to the text can be a useful way of determining which areas you know and which you don't.

Three ways of taking notes

1   Summarise the key points of a chapter

2   Make linear notes

A list of headings, subdivided with sub-headings listing the key points.

If you use linear notes, you can use different colours to highlight key points and keep topic areas together.

Use plenty of space to make your notes easy to use.

3   Try a diagrammatic form

The most common of which is a mind map.

To make a mind map, put the main heading in the centre of the paper and put a circle around it.

Draw lines radiating from this to the main sub-headings which again have circles around them.

Continue the process from the sub-headings to sub-sub-headings.

Highlighting and underlining

You may find it useful to underline or highlight key points in your study text – but do be selective.

You may also wish to make notes in the margins.

Revision phase

Kaplan has produced material specifically designed for your final examination preparation for this unit.

These include pocket revision notes and a bank of revision questions specifically in the style of the new syllabus.

Further guidance on how to approach the final stage of your studies is given in these materials.

Further reading

In addition to this text, you should also read the "Student section" of the "Accounting Technician" magazine every month to keep abreast of any guidance from the examiners.

TERMINOLOGY IAS AND UK GAAP

There are a number of differences in terminology between International and UK accounting practice.

This textbook uses the UK terminology but the IAS have been included in the brackets. The following table highlights the international equivalent of those terms that are different from that of the UK that you will see in this text.

The AAT have said that students need to be familiar with interchangeable terminology including IAS and UK GAAP.

Learners should expect to meet both UK and GAAP and IAS terms in the assessments.

Initially this will probably be limited to the financial statements but may be extended to other tasks in due course.

UK	International
Profit and loss account	Income statement
Balance sheet	Statement of financial position
Fixed assets	Non-current assets
Stock	Inventory
Debtors	Receivables
Creditors	Payables
VAT	Sales tax
Debtors ledger control account Sales ledger control account	Receivables ledger control account
Creditors ledger control account Purchase ledger control account	Payables ledger control account
Bad debt	Irrecoverable debt
Provision for doubtful debts	Allowance for receivables

Preparation of final accounts for a sole trader

Introduction

For Accounts Preparation II you need to be able to prepare the final accounts; a profit and loss account (income statement) and a balance sheet (statement of financial position) for a sole trader.

These final accounts may be prepared directly from the extended trial balance or from a trial balance plus various adjustments.

In this chapter we will consider the step by step approach to the final accounts preparation, firstly from an extended trial balance and then directly from an initial trial balance.

The knowledge for this unit has been acquired in Accounts Preparation I but within Accounts Preparation II, you will be expected to apply the skills to complete the final accounts.

KNOWLEDGE

Acquired from Accounts Preparation I

Identify reasons for closing off accounts and producing a trial balance (4.1)

Explain the process, and limitations, of preparing a set of final accounts from a trial balance (4.2)

SKILLS

Produce a trial balance from accounting information (2.1)

Prepare a profit and loss account (income statement) (2.2)

Prepare a balance sheet (statement of financial position) (2.3)

CONTENTS

1   The profit and loss (income statement) for a sole trader
2   The balance sheet (statement of financial position) for a sole trader
3   Preparing final accounts from the trial balance

1 The profit and loss account (income statement) for a sole trader

1.1 Introduction

In Accounts Preparation I we considered in outline the layout of a profit and loss account for a sole trader. Now we will consider it in more detail.

1.2 Trading, profit and loss account (income statement)

Technically the profit and loss account is split into two elements:

- the trading account;
- the profit and loss account.

However, in general the whole statement is referred to as the profit and loss account.

1.3 Trading account

The trading account calculates the gross profit or loss that has been made from the trading activities of the sole trader – the buying and selling of goods.

 Definition

The gross profit (or loss) is the profit (or loss) from the trading activities of the sole trader.

The trading account looks like this:

		£	£
Sales			X
Less:	Cost of sales		
	Opening stock	X	
	Purchases	X	
		X	
	Less: Closing stock	(X)	
			(X)
	Gross profit (loss)		X

1.4 Profit and loss account (income statement)

The remaining content of the profit and loss account is a list of the expenses of the business. These are deducted from the gross profit to give the net profit or loss.

Definition

The net profit or loss is the profit or loss after deduction of all of the expenses of the business.

Activity 1

Profit and loss account extract for the year ended 31 December 20X2.

Calculate the sales and cost of sales (complete the boxes).

	£	£
Sales		292,500
Less: Cost of sales		
Opening stock	37,500	
Purchases	158,700	
	196,200	
Less: Closing stock	(15,000)	
		181,200
Gross profit		111,300

A typical profit and loss account (income statement) is shown below.

Trading, profit and loss account of Stanley for the year ended 31 December 20X2

	£	£
Sales		X
Less: Cost of sales		
Stock on 1 January (opening stock)	X	
Add: Purchases of goods	X	
	―――	
	X	
Less: Stock on 31 December (closing stock)	(X)	
		(X)
		―――
Gross profit		X
Sundry income:		
Discounts received	X	
Commission received	X	
Rent received	X	
		X
		―――
		X
Less: Expenses:		
Rent	X	
Rates	X	
Lighting and heating	X	
Telephone	X	
Postage	X	
Insurance	X	
Stationery	X	
Payroll expenses	X	
Depreciation	X	
Accountancy and audit fees	X	
Bank charges and interest	X	
Irrecoverable debts	X	
Allowance for doubtful debts adjustment	X	
Delivery costs	X	
Van running expenses	X	
Selling expenses	X	
Discounts allowed	X	
	―――	(X)
		―――
Net profit/(Loss)		X/(X)
		―――

1.5 Preparation of the profit and loss account (income statement)

The trading and profit and loss account is prepared by listing all of the entries from the ETB that are in the profit and loss columns.

Example

Given below is the final ETB for Lyttleton

Account name	Trial balance		Adjustments		Profit and loss account		Balance sheet	
	DR £	CR £	DR £	CR £	DR £	CR £	DR £	CR £
Capital		7,830						7,830
Cash	2,010						2,010	
Fixed assets	9,420						9,420	
Accumulated depreciation		3,470		942				4,412
SLCA	1,830						1,830	
Opening stock	1,680				1,680			
PLCA		390						390
Sales		14,420				14,420		
Purchases	8,180			1,500	6,680			
Rent	1,100		100		1,200			
Electricity	940		400		1,340			
Rates	950			200	750			
Depreciation expense			942		942			
Allowance for doubtful debts adjustments			55		55			
Allowance for doubtful debts				55				55
Drawings			1,500				1,500	
Accruals				500				500
Prepayments			200				200	
Closing stock BS			1,140				1,140	
Closing stock P&L				1,140		1,140		
Profit (15,560 – 12,647)					2,913			2,913
	26,110	26,110	4,337	4,337	15,560	15,560	16,100	16,100

We will now show how the final profit and loss account for Lyttleton would look.

Solution

Trading and profit and loss account of Lyttleton for the year ended 31 December 20X5

			£	£
Sales				14,420
Less:	Cost of sales			
	Opening stock		1,680	
	Purchases		6,680	
			———	
			8,360	
Less:	Closing stock		(1,140)	
			———	(7,220)
				———
Gross profit				7,200
Less: Expenses				
	Rent		1,200	
	Electricity		1,340	
	Rates		750	
	Depreciation		942	
	Allowance for doubtful debts increase		55	
			———	
Total expenses				(4,287)
				———
Net profit				2,913
				———

All of the figures in the profit and loss columns have been used in the trading, profit and loss account.

The final net profit is the profit figure calculated as the balancing figure in the ETB.

2 The balance sheet (statement of financial position) for a sole trader

2.1 Introduction

Again we have considered a balance sheet in outline in an Accounts Preparation I and now we will consider it in more detail.

 Definition

A balance sheet (statement of financial position) is a list of the assets and liabilities of the sole trader at the end of the accounting period.

The assets are split into fixed assets and current assets.

 Definition

Fixed assets (non-current assets) are assets for long-term use within the business e.g. buildings.

 Definition

Current assets are assets that are either currently cash or will soon be converted into cash e.g. stock.

The liabilities are split into current liabilities and long term liabilities.

 Definition

Current liabilities are the short term creditors of the business. This generally means creditors who are due to be paid within twelve months of the balance sheet date e.g. trade creditors.

 Definition

Long-term liabilities (non-current liabilities) are creditors who will be paid after more than 12 months. These are deducted to give the net assets e.g. long term loans.

An example of a typical sole trader's balance sheet (statement of financial position) is given below:

Balance sheet of Stanley at 31 December 20X2

	Cost £	Depreciation £	£
Fixed assets			
Freehold factory	X	X	X
Machinery	X	X	X
Motor vehicles	X	X	X
	X	X	X
Current assets			
Stocks		X	
Trade debtors	X		
Less: Allowance for doubtful debts	(X)		
		X	
Prepayments		X	
Cash at bank		X	
Cash in hand		X	
		X	
Current liabilities			
Trade creditors	X		
Accruals	X		
		(X)	
Net current assets			X
Total assets less current liabilities			X
Long-term liabilities			
12% loan			(X)
Net assets			X
Capital at 1 January			X
Net profit for the year			X
			X
Less: Drawings			(X)
Proprietor's funds			X

2.2 Assets and liabilities

The assets and liabilities in a formal balance sheet are listed in a particular order:

- firstly the fixed assets less the accumulated depreciation (remember that this net total is known as the net book value);

- next the current assets in the following order – stock, debtors, prepayments then bank and cash balances;

- next the current liabilities – creditors and accruals that are payable within 12 months;

- finally the long-term creditors such as loan accounts;

The assets are all added together and the liabilities are then deducted. This gives the balance sheet total.

2.3 Capital balances

The total of the assets less liabilities of the sole trader should be equal to the capital of the sole trader.

The capital is shown in the balance sheet as follows:

	£
Opening capital at the start of the year	X
Add: Net profit/(loss) for the year	X
	X
Less: Drawings	(X)
Closing capital	X

This closing capital should be equal to the total of all of the assets less liabilities of the sole trader shown in the top part of the balance sheet.

Example

Given below is the completed ETB for Lyttleton. This time the balance sheet will be prepared.

Account name	Trial balance		Adjustments		Profit and loss account		Balance sheet	
	DR £	CR £	DR £	CR £	DR £	CR £	DR £	CR £
Capital		7,830						7,830
Cash	2,010						2,010	
Fixed assets	9,420						9,420	
Accumulated depreciation		3,470		942				4,412
SLCA	1,830						1,830	
Stock	1,680				1,680			
PLCA		390						390
Sales		14,420				14,420		
Purchases	8,180			1,500	6,680			
Rent	1,100		100		1,200			
Electricity	940		400		1,340			
Rates	950			200	750			
Depreciation expense			942		942			
Allowance for doubtful debts adjustments			55		55			
Allowance for doubtful debts				55				55
Drawings			1,500				1,500	
Accruals				500				500
Prepayments			200				200	
Closing stock – Profit and loss				1,140		1,140		
Closing stock – Balance sheet	,		1,140				1,140	
Profit (15,560 – 12,647)					2,913			2,913
	26,110	**26,110**	**4,337**	**4,337**	**15,560**	**15,560**	**16,100**	**16,100**

Each of the assets and liabilities that appear in the balance sheet columns will appear in the balance sheet.

Solution

Balance sheet of Lyttleton at 31 December 20X5

	Cost	Accumulated Dep'n	
	£	£	£
Fixed assets	9,420	4,412	5,008
Current assets			
Stocks		1,140	
Trade debtors	1,830		
Less: Allowance for doubtful debts	(55)		
		1,775	
Prepayments		200	
Cash		2,010	
		5,125	
Less:			
Current liabilities			
Creditors	390		
Accruals	500		
		(890)	
Net current assets			4,235
Net assets			9,243
Capital 1 January			7,830
Net profit for the year			2,913
			10,743
Less: Drawings			(1,500)
Proprietor's funds			9,243

Note

- the fixed assets are shown at their net book value;

- the current assets are sub-totalled as are the current liabilities – the current liabilities are then deducted from the current assets to give net current assets;

- the net current assets are added to the fixed asset net book value to reach the balance sheet total, net assets.

The balance sheet total of net assets should be equal to the closing capital; the balance sheet is then said to balance. If your balance sheet does not balance then make some quick obvious checks such as the adding up and that all figures have been included at the correct amount but do not spend too much time searching for your error as the time can be better used on the rest of the examination. If you have time left over at the end then you can check further for the difference.

 Activity 2

Given below is a completed extended trial balance.

Extended trial balance at 31 December 20X6

Account name	Trial balance DR £	Trial balance CR £	Adjustments DR £	Adjustments CR £	Profit and loss account DR £	Profit and loss account CR £	Balance sheet DR £	Balance sheet CR £
Fittings	7,300						7,300	
Accumulated depreciation 1.1.X6		2,500		400				2,900
Leasehold	30,000						30,000	
Accumulated depreciation 1.1.X6		6,000		1,000				7,000
Stock 1 January 20X6	15,000				15,000			
Sales ledger control account	10,000			500			9,500	
Allowance for doubtful debts 1.1.X6		800	515					285
Cash in hand	50						50	
Cash at bank	1,250						1,250	
Purchases ledger control account		18,000						18,000
Capital		19,050						19,050
Drawings	4,750		1,200				5,950	
Purchases	80,000			1,200	78,800			
Sales		120,000				120,000		
Wages	12,000			200	11,800			
Advertising	4,000		200		4,200			
Rates	1,800			360	1,440			
Bank charges	200				200			
Depreciation – Fittings			400		400			
Depreciation – Lease			1,000		1,000			

Allowance for doubtful debts adjustments				515		515		
Irrecoverable debts			500		500			
Prepayments			360				360	
Closing stock BS			21,000				21,000	
Closing stock P&L				21,000		21,000		
					113,340	141,515		
Net profit					28,175			28,175
	166,350	166,350	25,175	25,175	141,515	141,515	75,410	75,410

Prepare the profit and loss account for the business.

For items in italics, pick the appropriate account heading.

Profit and loss account for the year ended 31 December 20X6

	£	£
Sales		
Less: Cost of sales		
Opening stock/ Closing stock/ Purchases		
Purchases/ Opening stock/ Closing stock		
		____
Less: *Opening stock/ Closing stock/ Purchases*		____
		____
Gross profit		
Less: Expenses		
Trade debtors/Wages		
Advertising/ Prepayments		
Drawings/ Rates		
Bank charges/ Capital		
Depreciation/ Accumulated depreciation – F&F		
– lease		
Allowance for doubtful debts adjustment		
Irrecoverable debts		____
Total expenses		____
Net profit		____

Prepare the balance sheet for the business.

For items in italics, circle the appropriate account heading.

Prepare a balance sheet for the business.

Balance sheet as at 31 December 20X6

	£	£	£
Fixed assets:			
Fittings/ Closing stock			
Trade debtors/ Leasehold			
	_____	_____	_____
	_____	_____	
Current assets:			
Closing stock/ Opening stock			
Trade creditors/ Trade debtors			
Less: Allowance for doubtful debts			
	_____		
Accruals/ Prepayments			
Cash at bank/ Drawings			
Capital/ Cash in hand			
		_____	
Current liabilities:			
Trade debtors/ Trade creditors			
		_____	
			_____
			_____
Owner's capital			
Capital at 1.1.X6			
Drawings/ Net profit for the year			
Less: Capital/ Drawings			
			_____
			_____

KAPLAN PUBLISHING

3 Preparing final accounts from the trial balance

3.1 Introduction

As we have seen in Accounts Preparation I, the extended trial balance is a useful working paper for the eventual preparation of the final accounts of a sole trader. However, in the examination you may well be required to prepare a set of final accounts directly from the trial balance.

In this section we will work through a comprehensive example which will include the extraction of the initial trial balance, correction of errors and clearing a suspense account, accounting for year end adjustments and finally the preparation of the final accounts.

Example

Given below are the balances taken from a sole trader's ledger accounts on 31 March 20X4

	£
Sales ledger control account	30,700
Telephone	1,440
Purchases ledger control account	25,680
Heat and light	2,480
Motor vehicles at cost	53,900
Computer equipment at cost	4,500
Carriage inwards	1,840
Carriage outwards	3,280
Wages	67,440
Loan interest	300
Capital	48,000
Drawings	26,000
Allowance for doubtful debts	450
Bank overdraft	2,880
Purchases	126,800
Petty cash	50
Sales	256,400
Insurance	3,360
Accumulated depreciation – motor vehicles	15,000
Accumulated depreciation – computer equipment	2,640
Stock at 1 April 20X3	13,200
Loan	8,000
Rent	23,760

The following information is also available:

(i)   The value of stock at 31 March 20X4 was £14,400.

(ii)   Motor vehicles are to be depreciated at 30% on reducing balance basis and computer equipment at 20% on cost.

(iii)   A telephone bill for £180 for the three months to 31 March 20X4 did not arrive until after the trial balance had been drawn up.

(iv)   Of the insurance payments, £640 is for the year ending 31 March 20X5.

(v)   A irrecoverable debt of £700 is to be written off and an allowance of 2% is required against the remaining debtors.

Solution

Step 1

The first stage is to draw up the initial trial balance. Remember that assets and expenses are debit balances and liabilities and income are credit balances.

	£	£
Sales ledger control account	30,700	
Telephone	1,440	
Purchases ledger control account		25,680
Heat and light	2,480	
Motor vehicles at cost	53,900	
Computer equipment at cost	4,500	
Carriage inwards	1,840	
Carriage outwards	3,280	
Wages	67,440	
Loan interest	300	
Capital		48,000
Drawings	26,000	
Allowance for doubtful debts		450
Bank overdraft		2,880
Purchases	126,800	
Petty cash	50	
Sales		256,400
Insurance	3,360	
Accumulated depreciation – motor vehicles		15,000
Accumulated depreciation– computer equipment		2,640
Stock at 1 April 20X3	13,200	
Loan		8,000
Rent	23,760	
	359,050	359,050

Step 2

Now to deal with the year end adjustments:

(a)   The value of stock at 31 March 20X4 was £14,400.

Closing stock – profit and loss

	£		£
Balance c/d	14,400	Closing stock balance sheet	14,400

Closing stock – balance sheet

	£		£
Closing stock profit and loss	14,400		

- We now have the closing stock for the profit and loss account and in the balance sheet.

(b)   The motor vehicles and computer equipment have yet to be depreciated for the year. Motor vehicles are depreciated at 30% on reducing balance basis and computer equipment at 20% on cost.

Motor vehicles depreciation (53,900 – 15,000) × 30% = £11,670

Computer equipment depreciation 4,500 × 20% = £900

Depreciation expense account – motor vehicles

	£		£
Accumulated depreciation	11,670		

Accumulated depreciation account – motor vehicles

	£		£
		Balance b/d	15,000
Balance c/d	26,670	Depreciation expense	11,670
	26,670		26,670
		Balance b/d	26,670

Depreciation expense account – computer equipment

	£		£
Accumulated depreciation	900		

Accumulated depreciation account – computer equipment

	£		£
		Balance b/d	2,640
Balance c/d	3,540	Depreciation expense	900
	3,540		3,540
		Balance b/d	3,540

(c) A telephone bill for £180 for the three months to 31 March 20X4 did not arrive until after the trial balance had been drawn up.

This needs to be accrued for:

Debit	Telephone	£180
Credit	Accruals	£180

Telephone account

	£		£
Balance b/d	1,440		
Accrual	180	Balance c/d	1,620
	1,620		1,620
Balance b/d	1,620		

Accruals

	£		£
		Telephone	180

(d) Of the insurance payments £640 is for the year ending 31 March 20X5.

This must be adjusted for as a prepayment:

Debit	Prepayment	£640
Credit	Insurance account	£640

Prepayments

	£		£
Insurance	640		

Insurance account

	£		£
Balance b/d	3,360	Prepayment	640
		Balance c/d	2,720
	———		———
	3,360		3,360
	———		———
Balance b/d	2,720		

(e) An irrecoverable debt of £700 is to be written off and an allowance of 2% is required against the remaining debtors.

Firstly, the irrecoverable debt must be written off in order to find the amended balance on the sales ledger control account.

Debit   Irrecoverable debts expense   £700

Credit   Sales ledger control account   £700

Irrecoverable debts expense account

	£		£
Sales ledger control account	700		

Sales ledger control account

	£		£
Balance b/d	30,700	Irrecoverable debts expense	700
		Balance c/d	30,000
	———		———
	30,700		30,700
	———		———
Balance b/d	30,000		

Now we can determine the allowance for doubtful debts required at £30,000 × 2% = £600. The balance on the allowance account in the trial balance is £450, therefore an increase of £150 is required.

Debit   Allowance for doubtful debts adjustment   £150

Credit   Allowance for doubtful debts account   £150

Allowance for doubtful debts adjustment account

	£		£
Allowance for doubtful debts	150	Balance c/d	150
	150		150
Balance b/d	150		

Allowance for doubtful debts account

	£		£
		Balance b/d	450
Balance c/d	600	Allowance for doubtful debts adjustment	150
	600		600
		Balance b/d	600

Step 5

Now that all of the adjustments have been put through the ledger accounts, an amended trial balance can be drawn up as a check and as a starting point for preparing the final accounts. The amended and additional ledger accounts are all shown below.

Closing stock – profit and loss

	£		£
Balance c/d	14,400	Closing stock balance sheet	14,400
	14,400		14,400
		Balance b/d	14,400

Closing stock – balance sheet

	£		£
Closing stock profit and loss	14,400	Balance c/d	14,400
	14,400		14,400
Balance b/d	14,400		

Accumulated depreciation account – motor vehicles

	£		£
		Balance b/d	15,000
Balance c/d	26,670	Depreciation expense	11,670
	26,670		26,670
		Balance b/d	26,670

Depreciation expense account – motor vehicles

	£		£
Accumulated depreciation	11,670		

Depreciation expense account – computer equipment

	£		£
Accumulated depreciation	900		

Accumulated depreciation account – computer equipment

	£		£
		Balance b/d	2,640
Balance c/d	3,540	Depreciation expense	900
	3,540		3,540
		Balance b/d	3,540

Telephone account

	£		£
Balance b/d	1,440		
Accrual	180	Balance c/d	1,620
	1,620		1,620
Balance b/d	1,620		

Accruals

	£		£
		Telephone	180

Prepayments

	£		£
Insurance	640		

Insurance account

	£		£
Balance b/d	3,360	Prepayment	640
		Balance c/d	2,720
	———		———
	3,360		3,360
	———		———
Balance b/d	2,720		

Sales ledger control account

	£		£
Balance b/d	30,700	Irrecoverable debts expense	700
		Balance c/d	30,000
	———		———
	30,700		30,700
	———		———
Balance b/d	30,000		

Irrecoverable debts expense account

	£		£
Sales ledger control	700		
		Balance c/d	700
	———		———
	700		700
	———		———
Balance b/d	700		

Allowance for doubtful debts account

	£		£
		Balance b/d	450
Balance c/d	600	Allowance for doubtful debts adjustment	150
	———		———
	600		600
	———		———
		Balance b/d	600

Allowance for doubtful debts adjustment account

	£		£
Allowance for doubtful debts	150	Balance c/d	150
	_____		_____
	150		150
	_____		_____
Balance b/d	150		

Trial balance at 31 March 20X4

	£	£
Sales ledger control account	30,000	
Telephone	1,620	
Purchases ledger control account		25,680
Heat and light	2,480	
Motor vehicles at cost	53,900	
Computer equipment at cost	4,500	
Carriage inwards	1,840	
Carriage outwards	3,280	
Wages	67,440	
Loan interest	300	
Capital		48,000
Drawings	26,000	
Allowance for doubtful debts		600
Bank overdraft		2,880
Purchases	126,800	
Petty cash	50	
Sales		256,400
Insurance	2,720	
Accumulated depreciation – motor vehicles		26,670
Accumulated depreciation – computer equipment		3,540
Stock at 1 April 20X3	13,200	
Loan		8,000
Rent	23,760	
Stock at 31 March 20X4	14,400	14,400
Depreciation expense – motor vehicles	11,670	
Depreciation expense – computer equipment	900	
Accruals		180
Prepayments	640	
Allowance for doubtful debt adjustment	150	
Irrecoverable debts expense	700	
	_____	_____
	386,350	386,350
	_____	_____

Step 6

We are now in a position to prepare the final accounts for the sole trader. Take care with the carriage inwards and carriage outwards. They are both expenses of the business but carriage inwards is treated as part of cost of sales, whereas carriage outwards is one of the list of expenses.

Profit and loss account for the year ended 31 March 20X4

	£	£
Sales		256,400
Less: Cost of sales		
Opening stock	13,200	
Carriage inwards	1,840	
Purchases	126,800	
	141,840	
Less: Closing stock	(14,400)	
		127,440
Gross profit		128,960
Less: Expenses		
Telephone	1,620	
Heat and light	2,480	
Carriage outwards	3,280	
Wages	67,440	
Loan interest	300	
Insurance	2,720	
Rent	23,760	
Depreciation expense – motor vehicles	11,670	
Depreciation expense – computer equipment	900	
Irrecoverable debts	700	
Allowance for doubtful debts adjustment	150	
Total expenses		115,020
Net profit		13,940

Balance sheet as at 31 March 20X4

	Cost £	Accumulated depreciation £	Net book value £
Fixed assets			
Motor vehicles	53,900	26,670	27,230
Computer equipment	4,500	3,540	960
	58,400	30,210	28,190
Current assets			
Stock		14,400	
Trade debtors	30,000		
Less: Allowance for doubtful debts	(600)		
		29,400	
Prepayment		640	
Petty cash		50	
		44,490	
Current liabilities			
Bank overdraft	2,880		
Trade Creditors	25,680		
Accruals	180		
		28,740	
Net current assets			15,750
Total assets less current liabilities			43,940
Long term liability:			
Loan			(8,000)
Net assets			35,940
Capital			
Opening capital			48,000
Net profit for the year			13,940
			61,940
Less: Drawings			26,000
Proprietor's funds			35,940

Activity 3

Given below is the list of ledger balances for a sole trader at 30 June 20X4 after all of the year end adjustments have been put through.

	£
Sales	165,400
Sales ledger control account	41,350
Wages	10,950
Bank	1,200
Rent	8,200
Capital	35,830
Purchases ledger control account	15,100
Purchases	88,900
Electricity	1,940
Telephone	980
Drawings	40,000
Stock at 1 July 20X3	9,800
Motor vehicles at cost	14,800
Accumulated depreciation – motor vehicles	7,800
Fixtures at cost	3,200
Accumulated depreciation – fittings	1,800
Accruals	100
Prepayments	210
Stock at 30 June 20X4 – balance sheet	8,300
Stock at 30 June 20X4 – profit and loss	8,300
Depreciation expense – motor vehicles	3,700
Depreciation expense – fittings	800

You are required to:

(i)   Draw up a trial balance to check that it balances (you should find that the trial balance does balance).

(ii) Prepare the final accounts for the sole trader for the year ending 30 June 20X4.

(i)   **Trial balance as at 30 June 20X4**

	£	£
Sales		
Sales ledger control account		
Wages		
Bank		
Rent		
Capital		
Purchases ledger control account		
Purchases		
Electricity		
Telephone		
Drawings		
Stock at 1 July 20X3		
Motor vehicles at cost		
Accumulated depreciation – motor vehicles		
Fixtures at cost		
Accumulated depreciation – fittings		
Accruals		
Prepayments		
Stock at 30 June 20X4 – balance sheet		
Stock at 30 June 20X4 – profit and loss		
Depreciation expense – motor vehicles		
Depreciation expense – fittings		
	234,330	234,330

(ii)   **Profit and loss account for the year ending 30 June 20X4**

	£	£
Sales		
Less: Cost of sales		
	____	
Less:		
	____	
		____
Gross profit		

Less: Expenses

Total expenses

Net profit

Balance sheet as at 30 June 20X4

	Cost £	Depreciation £	NBV £
Fixed assets			
	_____	_____	_____
	_____	_____	_____
Current assets			
		_____	
Current liabilities			
		_____	
Net current assets			
Net assets			44,260
			_____
Capital			
Net profit for the year			
			_____
Drawings			
			_____
Proprietor's funds			44,260

Activity 4

Tick as appropriate.

1   Opening stock is recorded in the profit and loss account as

   An expense ☐

   Cost of sales ☐

2   Indicate where the drawings should be shown in the final accounts

   Profit and loss expenses ☐

   Balance sheet as a deduction to capital ☐

3   Payroll expenses are recorded as

   A liability in the balance sheet ☐

   An expense in the profit and loss account ☐

4   Does the allowance for doubtful debt adjustment appear in the profit and loss account or balance sheet?

   Profit and loss account ☐

   Balance sheet ☐

5   The irrecoverable debts are recorded in the balance sheet as a deduction from trade debtors

   True ☐

   False ☐

4 Summary

The Accounts Preparation II unit requires the preparation of the final accounts for a sole trader.

The profit and loss account (income statement) for the period summarises the transactions in the period and leads to a net profit or loss for the period.

The balance sheet (statement of financial position) lists the assets and liabilities of the business on the last day of the accounting period in a particular order.

If you have to prepare the final accounts from an extended trial balance then each balance will already have been classified as either a profit and loss account item or a balance sheet item.

If you are preparing the final accounts from a trial balance, you will have to recognise whether the balances should appear in the profit and loss account or in the balance sheet.

Answers to chapter activities

Activity 1

Profit and loss account extract for the year ended 31 December 20X2

Calculate the sales and cost of sales.

	£	£
Sales		292,500
Less: Cost of sales		
Opening stock	37,500	
Purchases	158,700	
	196,200	
Less: Closing stock	(15,000)	
		(181,200)
Gross profit		111,300

Activity 2

Profit and loss account for the year ended 31 December 20X6

	£	£
Sales		120,000
Less: Cost of sales		
Opening stock	15,000	
Purchases	78,800	
	93,800	
Less: Closing stock	(21,000)	
		(72,800)
Gross profit		47,200

Less: Expenses

Wages		11,800
Advertising		4,200
Rates		1,440
Bank charges		200
Depreciation – F&F		400
– lease		1,000
Allowance for doubtful debts adjustment		(515)
Irrecoverable debts		500

Total expenses	(19,025)
Net profit	28,175

Balance sheet as at 31 December 20X6

	£	£	£
Fixed assets			
Fittings	7,300	2,900	4,400
Leasehold	30,000	7,000	23,000
	37,300	9,900	27,400
Current assets			
Stock		21,000	
Trade debtors	9,500		
Less: Allowance for doubtful debts	(285)		
		9,215	
Prepayments		360	
Cash at bank		1,250	
Cash in hand		50	
		31,875	
Current liabilities			
Trade creditors		(18,000)	
Net current assets			13,875
Net assets			41,275
Owner's capital			
Capital at 1.1.X6			19,050
Net profit for the year			28,175
Less: Drawings			(5,950)
Proprietor's funds			41,275

Activity 3

(i) **Trial balance as at 30 June 20X4**

	£	£
Sales		165,400
Sales ledger control account	41,350	
Wages	10,950	
Bank	1,200	
Rent	8,200	
Capital		35,830
Purchases ledger control account		15,100
Purchases	88,900	
Electricity	1,940	
Telephone	980	
Drawings	40,000	
Stock at 1 July 20X3	9,800	
Motor vehicles at cost	14,800	
Accumulated depreciation – motor vehicles		7,800
Fixtures at cost	3,200	
Accumulated depreciation – fittings		1,800
Accruals		100
Prepayments	210	
Stock at 30 June 20X4 – profit and loss		8,300
Stock at 30 June 20X4 – balance sheet	8,300	
Depreciation expense – motor vehicles	3,700	
Depreciation expense – fittings	800	
	234,330	234,330

(ii) **Profit and loss account for the year ending 30 June 20X4**

	£	£
Sales		165,400
Less: Cost of sales		
Opening stock	9,800	
Purchases	88,900	
	98,700	
Less: Closing stock	(8,300)	
		(90,400)
Gross profit		75,000

Less: Expenses

Wages	10,950
Rent	8,200
Electricity	1,940
Telephone	980
Depreciation – motor vehicles	3,700
Depreciation – fittings	800

Total expenses	26,570
Net profit	48,430

Balance sheet as at 30 June 20X4

	Cost £	Depreciation £	NBV £
Fixed assets			
Motor vehicles	14,800	7,800	7,000
Fittings	3,200	1,800	1,400
	18,000	9,600	8,400
Current assets			
Stock		8,300	
Trade debtors		41,350	
Prepayments		210	
Bank		1,200	
		51,060	
Current liabilities			
Trade creditors	15,100		
Accruals	100		
		(15,200)	
Net current assets			35,860
Net assets			44,260
Capital			35,830
Net profit for the year			48,430
			84,260
Drawings			(40,000)
Proprietor's funds			44,260

Activity 4

1   Opening stock is recorded in the profit and loss account as

     Cost of sales

2   Indicate where the drawings should be shown in the final accounts

     Balance sheet

3   Payroll expenses are recorded as

     An expense in the profit and loss account

4   Does the allowance for doubtful debt adjustment appear in the profit and loss account or balance sheet?

     Profit and loss

5   The irrecoverable debts are recorded in the balance sheet as a deduction from trade debtors

     False

5 Test your knowledge

 Workbook Activity 5

David Pedley

The following information is available for David Pedley's business for the year ended 31 December 20X8. He started his business on 1 January 20X8.

	£
Creditors	6,400
Debtors	5,060
Purchases	16,100
Sales	28,400
Motor van	1,700
Drawings	5,100
Insurance	174
General expenses	1,596
Rent and rates	2,130
Salaries	4,162
Stock at 31 December 20X8	2,050
Sales returns	200
Cash at bank	2,628
Cash in hand	50
Capital introduced	4,100

Required:

Prepare a profit and loss account for the year ended 31 December 20X8 and a balance sheet at that date.

Workbook Activity 6

Karen Finch

On 1 April 20X7 Karen Finch started a business with capital of £10,000 which she paid into a business bank account.

The following is a summary of the cash transactions for the first year.

	£
Amounts received from customers	17,314
Salary of assistant	2,000
Cash paid to suppliers for purchases	10,350
Purchase of motor van on 31 March 20X8	4,000
Drawings during the year	2,400
Amounts paid for electricity	560
Rent and rates for one year	1,100
Postage and stationery	350

At the end of the year, Karen was owed £4,256 by her customers and owed £5,672 to her suppliers. She has promised her assistant a bonus for the year of £400. At 31 March 20X8 this had not been paid.

At 31 March 20X8 there were stocks of £4,257 and the business owed £170 for electricity for the last quarter of the year. A year's depreciation is to be charged on the motor van at 25% on cost.

Required:

Prepare a profit and loss account for the year ended 31 March 20X8 and a balance sheet at that date.

Workbook Activity 7

The trial balance of Elmdale at 31 December 20X8 is as follows

	DR £	CR £
Capital		8,602
Stock	2,700	
Sales		21,417
Purchases	9,856	
Rates	1,490	
Drawings	4,206	
Electricity	379	
Freehold shop	7,605	
Debtors	2,742	
Creditors		3,617
Cash at bank		1,212
Cash in hand	66	
Sundry expenses	2,100	
Wages and salaries	3,704	
	34,848	34,848

In addition, Elmdale provides the following information:

(a) Closing stock has been valued for accounts purposes at £3,060.

(b) An electricity bill amounting to £132 in respect of the quarter to 28 February 20X9 was paid on 7 March 20X9.

(c) Rates include a payment of £1,260 made on 10 April 20X8 in respect of the year to 31 March 20X9.

Tasks

(a) Show the adjustments to the ledger accounts for the end-of-period adjustments (a) to (c).

(b) Prepare a trading and profit and loss account for the year ended 31 December 20X8.

Partnership accounts

2

Introduction

For Accounts Preparation II you need to apply acquired knowledge and skills from Accounts Preparation I and prepare a set of partnership accounts.

You need to be able to prepare a profit and loss account (income statement) for a partnership, which is basically the same as that for a sole trader, then prepare a partnership appropriation account and a balance sheet (statement of financial position) for the partnership.

You also need to be able to deal with events such as the admission of a new partner or the retirement of an old partner.

All of this will be dealt with in this chapter.

KNOWLEDGE
Describe the key components of a partnership agreement (1.1)
Identify and describe the key components of partnership accounts (1.2)
Profit and loss account (income statement)
Partnership appropriation account
Goodwill
Partners current accounts
Partners capital accounts
Balance sheet (statement of financial position)

CONTENTS

1 Accounting for partner's capital and profits
2 Appropriation of profit
3 Changes in the partnership agreement
4 Admission of a new partner
5 Retirement of a partner
6 Preparing final accounts for a partnership

SKILLS

Prepare the profit and loss (income statement) appropriation account for a partnership (2.1)

Accurately determine the allocation of profit to the partners after allowing for interest on capital, interest on drawings and any salary paid to partner(s) (2.2)

Prepare the current accounts for each partner and calculate the Balance c/d (2.3)

Record accurately the Balance c/ds on each partner's capital and current accounts, including drawings (3.1)

Prepare a balance sheet (statement of financial position) for a partnership, in compliance with the partnership agreement (3.2)

1 Accounting for partner's capital and profits

1.1 What is a partnership?

 Definition

A partnership is where two or more people carry on business together with a view to making a profit and sharing that profit.

In a partnership each of the partners will introduce capital into the business and each partner will have a share in the profits of the business.

1.2 Partnership capital

Each of the partners in a partnership will pay capital into the business in just the same way that a sole trader does.

In a partnership accounting system it is important to keep the capital paid in by each partner separate so that there is a record of how much the business owes back to each of the partners.

In order to keep a record of the capital paid in by each partner a separate capital account for each partner is kept in the main ledger.

 Definition

A capital account in a partnership is an account for each partner which records the capital that they have paid into the business.

When a partner pays capital into the business the double entry is:

DR Bank account

CR Partners' capital account

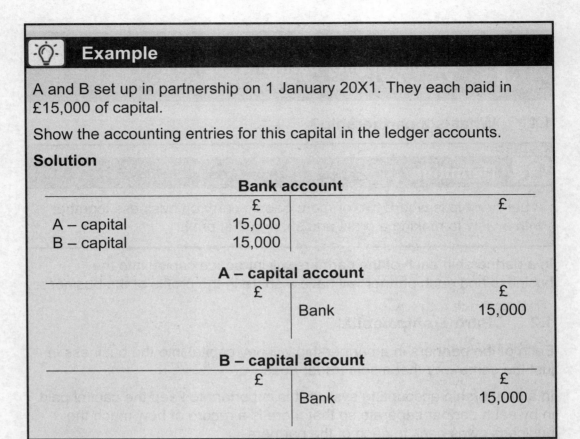

Example

A and B set up in partnership on 1 January 20X1. They each paid in £15,000 of capital.

Show the accounting entries for this capital in the ledger accounts.

Solution

Bank account

	£		£
A – capital	15,000		
B – capital	15,000		

A – capital account

	£		£
		Bank	15,000

B – capital account

	£		£
		Bank	15,000

1.3 Partnership profits

When a partnership makes a profit or a loss for an accounting period then this must be shared between the partners.

Usually there will be a partnership agreement which sets out what percentage of the profit each partner is to receive.

If there is no written partnership agreement then the Partnership Act 1890 states that profits should be shared equally between all of the partners.

1.4 Accounting for partnership profits

The profit that each partner is due from the business is recorded in his current account.

 ## Definition

The partners' current accounts record the amount of profit that is due to each partner from the business.

A separate current account that records the profit due to that partner is normally kept.

> ### Example
>
> A and B, from the previous example, earn £20,000 of profit for the year 20X1. The partnership agreement is to share this profit equally. Show their current accounts for the year 20X1.
>
> **Solution**
>
> **A – current account**
>
> | £ | | £ |
> |---|---|---|
> | | Profit for year | 10,000 |
>
> **B – current account**
>
> | £ | | £ |
> |---|---|---|
> | | Profit for year | 10,000 |
>
> **Trial balance extract**
>
> | | | Dr | Cr |
> |---|---|---|---|
> | Capital accounts | – A | | 15,000 |
> | | – B | | 15,000 |
> | Current accounts | – A | | 10,000 |
> | | – B | | 10,000 |
>
> Both the capital accounts and current accounts are credit balances as these are amounts owed back to the partners by the business, i.e. special creditors of the business.

1.5 Drawings

Just as a sole trader takes money and/or goods out of the business, in just the same way partners will do the same. The accounting entries for a partner's drawings are:

DR Partner's current account
CR Bank account

It is the partner's current account that is charged with the drawings.

Example

In the year 20X1 partner A had drawings of £6,000 and partner B drawings of £8,000. Show how these transactions would appear in the current accounts of the partners and what balances would be shown in the trial balance.

Solution

A – current account

	£		£
Drawings	6,000	Profit for year	10,000
Balance c/d	4,000		
	10,000		10,000
		Balance b/d	4,000

B – current account

	£		£
Drawings	8,000	Profit for year	10,000
Balance c/d	2,000		
	10,000		10,000
		Balance b/d	2,000

Trial balance extract

	Dr	Cr
Capital accounts – A		15,000
– B		15,000
Current accounts – A		4,000
– B		2,000

1.6 Columnar accounts

In some partnerships the ledger accounts for capital and current accounts are produced in columnar form which means that each partner has a column in a joint capital and current account.

Example

Using the example of A and B above we will see how their capital and current accounts would look if the ledger accounts were in columnar form.

Solution

Capital accounts

	A £	B £		A £	B £
			Bank	15,000	15,000

Current accounts

	A £	B £		A £	B £
Drawings	6,000	8,000	Profit for year	10,000	10,000
Balance c/d	4,000	2,000			
	10,000	10,000		10,000	10,000
			Balance b/d	4,000	2,000

Remember that the capital account is only used for recording the capital paid into the business by each partner. The profit earned and the drawings made by each partner are recorded in the current accounts.

The AAT has stated that questions in the examinations will be based on partnerships with no more than three partners therefore there should be plenty of room to use columnar accounts for capital and current accounts.

Activity 1

Continuing with the partnership of A and B, in the year 20X2 A paid a further £5,000 of capital into the business.

The profit of the business for the year was £28,000 and this is to be shared equally between A and B.

During the year A had cash drawings of £12,000 and B had cash drawings of £13,000.

Record these transactions in the capital and current accounts of A and B and show the balances on these accounts that would appear in the trial balance at the end of 20X2.

Capital account – A

	£		£
		Balance b/d	15,000
	___		___
	___		___

Capital account – B

	£		£
		Balance b/d	15,000
	___		___
	___		___

Current account – A

	£		£
		Balance b/d	4,000
	___		___
	___		___

Current account – B

	£			£
			Balance b/d	2,000
	——			——
	——			——

Trial balance extract

	Dr £	Cr £
Capital account – A		
Capital account – B		
Current account – A		
Current account – B		

1.7 Debit balances on current accounts

In some instances a partner may withdraw more in cash drawings than is owing to him out of accumulated profits. In this case the partner's current account will show a debit balance.

Example

Suppose that the balance on a partner's current account at the start of the year is a credit balance of £3,000.

His share of profit for the year is £17,000 and he has £22,000 of drawings.

Show the partner's current account for the year.

Solution

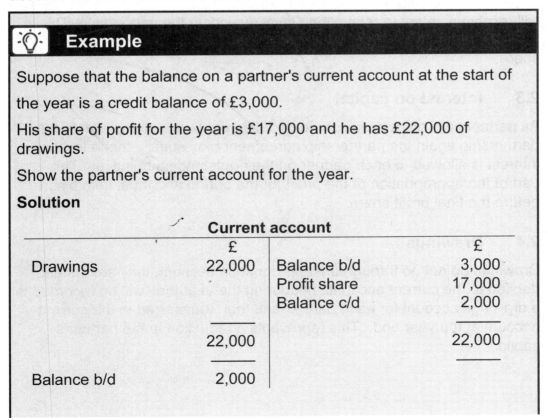

Current account

	£		£
Drawings	22,000	Balance b/d	3,000
		Profit share	17,000
		Balance c/d	2,000
	——		——
	22,000		22,000
	——		——
Balance b/d	2,000		

The balance on the current account is a debit balance and would be shown in the trial balance as such.

Always assume that any balances given for partners' current accounts are credit balances unless you are specifically told otherwise.

2 Appropriation of profit

2.1 Appropriation account

We have already seen how the profit of a partnership business is split between the partners in the business according to their profit sharing ratio and is credited to their current accounts.

The actual splitting up of the profit is done in a profit appropriation account. This can either take the form of another ledger account or it can be shown vertically.

2.2 Salaries

In some partnership agreements it is specified that one or more partners will receive a salary to reflect their level of work in the partnership. This is part of the appropriation of profit and must take place before the profit share.

2.3 Interest on capital

As partners will often have contributed different levels of capital into the partnership again the partnership agreement may specify that a level of interest is allowed to each partner on their outstanding balances. This is part of the appropriation of the profit for the period and must take place before the final profit share.

2.4 Drawings

Drawings do not go through the appropriation account, they are instead debited to the current accounts but during the year they will be recorded in a drawings account for each partner and then transferred to the current account at the year end. This represents a reduction in the partner's capital.

A proforma appropriation account is shown below for a partnership with three partners A, B and C for the year ended 31 12 20X7.

All the numbers are assumed.

	Year ended 31 Dec 20X7 £	Total £
Net profit		100,000
Salaries		
A	(10,000)	(10,000)
B	(15,000)	(15,000)
C	Nil	
Interest on capital		
A	(5,000)	(5,000)
B	(7,000)	(7,000)
C	(3,000)	(3,000)
Profit available for distribution		60,000
Profit share		
A	(30,000)	(30,000)
B	(20,000)	(20,000)
C	(10,000)	(10,000)
Balance		Nil

Note

1   There are three categories of appropriations that can be entered into the appropriation account

   (a)   Salaries

   (b)   Interest on capital

   (c)   Profit share

2   If any of the three categories change during the year then it is easier to have two columns for the periods when the change takes place which are then totalled in the total column. The column headings might look as follows.

	1 Jan 20 X7 to 30 Sept 20X7	1 Oct 20X7 to 31 Dec 20X7	Total

We shall study an example of this later in the chapter.

Example

X, Y and Z are in partnership sharing profits in the ratio 3:2:1

The profits for the year to 30 June 20X7 were £100,000.

Z receives a salary of £12,000 per annum.

The partners' capital accounts have balance b/d of £50,000, £30,000 and £10,000 respectively. Interest for the year is calculated as 5% of the capital balance b/d.

Produce the appropriation account for the year.

Solution

	Year ended 30 June 20X7 £	Total £
Net profit		100,000
Salaries:		
X		
Y		
Z	(12,000)	(12,000)
Interest on capital		
X (50,000 × 5%)	(2,500)	(2,500)
Y (30,000 × 5%)	(1,500)	(1,500)
Z (10,000 × 5%)	(500)	(500)
Profit available for distribution		83,500
Profit share		
X (83,500 × 3/6)	(41,750)	(41,750)
Y (83,500 × 2/6)	(27,833)	(27,833)
Z (83,500 × 1/6)	(13,917)	(13,917)
Balance		Nil

 Example

A and B are in partnership sharing profits equally and, for the year 20X1, the partnership made a profit of £20,000.

We will show how the partnership profit is appropriated in both a ledger appropriation account and a vertical appropriation account.

Solution

Ledger appropriation account

The net profit of the partnership is shown as a credit balance, amount owing to the partners, in the appropriation account.

Appropriation account

	£		£
		Balance b/d	20,000

A journal entry will then be put through for the split of the profit.

Debit Appropriation account – A's profit	£10,000
Debit Appropriation account – B's profit	£10,000

Credit A's current account	£10,000
Credit B's current account	£10,000

The appropriation account and the current accounts can then be written up:

Appropriation account

	£		£
Current account – A	10,000	Balance b/d	20,000
Current account – B	10,000		
	———		———
	20,000		20,000
	———		———

Current accounts

	A £	B £		A £	B £
			Appropriation account	£10,000	£10,000

Vertical appropriation account

	£
Net profit for the year	20,000
	———
Profit share – A	10,000
Profit share – B	10,000
	———
	20,000
	———

Example

C and D are in partnership and their capital balances are £100,000 and £60,000 respectively.

During 20X4 the profit made by the partnership totalled £80,000.

The partnership agreement specifies the following:

- D receives a salary of £15,000 per annum.
- Both partners receive interest on their capital balances at a rate of 5%.
- The profit sharing ratio is 2 : 1.

We will now appropriate the profit and write up the partners' current accounts.

C made £37,000 of drawings during the year and D made £33,500 of drawings during the year.

The Balance b/ds on their current accounts were both £1,000 credit balances.

Solution

The salary and the interest on capital must be deducted first from the available profits.

The remainder is then split in the profit share ratio of 2:1.

This means that C gets two thirds of the remaining profit whilst D gets one third of the remaining profit.

Appropriation account

		£	£
Profit for the year			80,000
Salary	– D	15,000	
Interest	– C (100,000 × 5%)	5,000	
	D (60,000 × 5%)	3,000	
			(23,000)
Profit available for profit share			57,000
Profit share	– C (57,000 × 2/3)		38,000
	D (57,000 × 1/3)		19,000
			57,000

The current accounts can now be written up to reflect the profit share and the drawings for the year.

Current account

	C £	D £		C £	D £
Drawings	37,000	33,500	Balance b/d	1,000	1,000
			Salary		15,000
			Interest on capital	5,000	3,000
Balance b/d	7,000	4,500	Profit share	38,000	19,000
	44,000	38,000		44,000	38,000
			Balance c/d	7,000	4,500

 Activity 2

Nick and Ted are in partnership sharing profits in the ratio of 3 : 2. During the year ending 30 June 20X4 the partnership made a profit of £120,000.

The partnership agreement states that Ted is to receive a salary of £20,000 and that interest on capital balances is paid at 6% per annum.

The balances on the current accounts, capital accounts and drawings accounts at the year end before the appropriation of profit were as follows:

		£
Capital	– Nick	150,000
	Ted	100,000
Current	– Nick	3,000 (credit)
	Ted	1,000 (debit)
Drawings	– Nick	56,000
	Ted	59,000

Complete the appropriation account and the partners' current accounts after appropriation of profit and transfer of drawings at 30 June 20X4.

Appropriation account

	£	£
Net profit		
Salary – Ted		
Interest on capital – Nick		
Ted		
	————	
		————
Profit available		
		————
Profit share – Nick		
Ted		
		————
		————

Current accounts

	Nick £	Ted £		Nick £	Ted £
Balance b/d			Balance b/d		
Drawings			Salary		
			Interest on capital		
Balance c/d			Profit share		
	———	———		———	———
	———	———		———	———
			Balance b/d		

2.5 Partnership losses

Any salaries and interest on capital must be appropriated first to the partners even if the partnership makes a loss or if this appropriation turns a profit into a loss.

Then the loss itself is split between the partners in the profit share ratio by debiting their current accounts.

KAPLAN PUBLISHING

Example

The partnership of E and F made a profit of £10,000 for the year ending 31 March 20X5.

The partnership agreement states that each partner receives interest on their capital balances of 10% per annum and that E receives a salary of £8,000.

Any remaining profits or losses are split in the ratio of 3 : 1.

The balances on their capital accounts were £50,000 and £40,000 respectively and neither partner had an Balance b/d on their current accounts.

Neither partner made any drawings during the year.

Write up the partnership profit appropriation account and the partners' current accounts for the year.

Appropriation account

		£	£
Partnership profit			10,000
Salary	– E	8,000	
Interest	– E	5,000	
	F	4,000	
		———	(17,000)
Loss to be shared			(7,000)
			———
Loss share	– E (7,000 × 3/4)		(5,250)
	F (7,000 × 1/4)		(1,750)
			———
			(7,000)
			———

Current account

	E £	F £		E £	F £
Loss share	5,250	1,750	Salary	8,000	
Balance c/d	7,750	2,250	Interest	5,000	4,000
	———	———		———	———
	13,000	4,000		13,000	4,000
	———	———		———	———
			Balance b/d	7,750	2,250

Example

A and B each have current account balances of £10,000.

During 20X1 A had drawings of £6,000 and B had drawings of £8,000.

Show how these are entered in the ledger accounts.

Solution

At the year end the drawings accumulated in the drawings accounts are transferred by a journal entry to the current accounts of the partners as follows:

Debit Current account – A	£6,000	
Debit Current account – B	£8,000	
Credit Drawings account – A		£6,000
Credit Drawings account – B		£8,000

Drawings account – A

	£		£
Cash	6,000	Current account	6,000

Drawings account – B

	£		£
Cash	8,000	Current account	8,000

Current accounts

	A £	B £		A £	B £
Drawings	6,000	8,000	Balance b/d		
				10,000	10,000

3 Changes in the partnership agreement

3.1 Changes in profit share

In some partnerships the partners will decide to change the partnership agreement and the profit share ratio part of the way through the year. In these cases the appropriation of profit must take place in two separate calculations.

Firstly, the profit for the period under the old profit share agreement must be appropriated using the old profit share ratio.

Secondly, the profit for the period after the change must be appropriated using the new profit share ratio.

 Example

Bill and Ben are in partnership and the profits of the partnership for the year ending 31 December 20X3 were £60,000.

The partnership agreement at the start of the year was that profits were to be shared equally.

However, on 31 March 20X3 it was decided to change the partnership agreement so that Ben received a salary of £8,000 per annum and the remaining profits were shared in the ratio of 2 : 1.

Both partners had an balance b/d on their current accounts of £2,000 (credit) and the profits for the year accrued evenly.

Show the appropriation of the profits to the partners' current accounts for the year.

Solution

Step 1

Determine the profit for the first three months of the year and appropriate that according to the old profit share ratio.

	£
Profit (£60,000 × 3/12)	15,000
	———
Bill (15,000 × 1/2)	7,500
Ben (15,000 × 1/2)	7,500
	———
	15,000
	———

Step 2

Determine the profit for the final nine months of the year and appropriate that according to the new profit share ratio.

Profit (£60,000 × 9/12)	45,000
Salary – Ben (£8,000 × 9/12)	(6,000)
Profit to be appropriated	39,000
Profit share – Bill (£39,000 × 2/3)	26,000
Ben (£39,000 × 1/3)	13,000
	39,000

Example

Consider the previous example and write up the appropriation account for the same information in a columnar form

Solution

	1 Jan – 31 Mar 2003	1 Apr – 31 Dec 2003	Total (£)
Profit	**15,000**	**45,000**	**60,000**
Salary			
Ben (£8,000 × 9/12)		6,000	6,000
Profit available for distribution	**15,000**	**39,000**	**54,000**
Profit share			
Bill	7,500	26,000	33,500
Ben	7,500	13,000	20,500
Balance	**Nil**	**Nil**	**Nil**

3.2   Changes in interest

The partnership agreement may be changed during a period so that for example a different rate of interest is paid on capital from a given date in the year.

The profit must be divided into the two periods and interest must be calculated both before and after that date.

KAPLAN PUBLISHING

Example

A, B and C are in partnership for the year ended 31 December 20X8, sharing profits in the ratio 3:2:1. The net profit for the year was £90,000.

At 1 January 20X8 the partners' capital was

	£
A	50,000
B	30,000
C	20,000

For the period to 30 April 20X8, the partners received interest at 3% on their capital at the beginning of the year. For the remainder of the year they received interest at 4% on their capital at the beginning of the year.

Task 1

Complete the table showing the interest received by the partners during the year for the two separate periods and in total

	1 Jan 08 – 30 Apr 08 £	1 May 08 – 31 Dec 08 £	Total £

Task 2

Prepare the appropriation account for the year to 31 December 2008.

Solution

Task 1

	1 Jan 08 – 30 Apr 08 £	1 May 08 – 31 Dec 08 £	Total £
Interest			
A	50,000 × 3% × 4/12 = 500	50,000 × 4% × 8/12 = 1,333	1,833
B	30,000 × 3% × 4/12 = 300	30,000 × 4% × 8/12 = 800	1,100
C	20,000 × 3% × 4/12 = 200	20,000 × 4% × 8/12 = 533	733

Task 2

Appropriation account for the year to 31 December 2008

	1 Jan 08 – 30 Apr 08 £	1 May 08 – 31 Dec 08 £	Total £
Net profit	**30,000**	**60,000**	**90,000**
A	500	1,333	1,833
B	300	800	1,100
C	200	533	733
Profit available for distribution	**29,000**	**57,334**	**86,334**
Profit share			
A	29,000 × 3/6 = 14,500	57,334 × 3/6 = 28,667	43,167
B	29,000 × 2/6 = 9,667	57,334 × 2/6 = 19,111	28,778
C	29,000 × 1/6 = 4,833	57,334 × 1/6 = 9,556	14,389
Balance	**Nil**	**Nil**	**Nil**

Activity 3

During the year ending 30 June 20X4, the partnership of Jill, Jane and Jan made a profit of £100,000.

Up until 31 March 20X4 the profit share ratio was 2 : 2 : 1

However, the partnership agreement was changed on 31 March 20X4 so that Jane was to receive a salary of £16,000 per annum and that the profits were to be shared equally.

The balances on the partners' current accounts and drawings accounts at 30 June 20X4 were as follows:

			£
Current accounts	–	Jill	3,000
		Jane	2,000
		Jan	1,000
Drawings accounts	–	Jill	38,000
		Jane	40,000
		Jan	25,000

Prepare the appropriation account and the partners' current accounts for the year.

Appropriation account   £
Profit to 31 March 20X4

Profit share   –   Jill
                       Jane
                       Jan
                                                        ———

                                                        ———

Profit to 30 June 20X4
Salary   Jane
                                                        ———
Profit available
                                                        ———
Profit share   –   Jill
                       Jane
                       Jan
                                                        ———

                                                        ———

	Current accounts						
	Jill	Jane	Jan		Jill	Jane	Jan
	£	£	£		£	£	£
Drawings				Balance b/d			
				Profit share			
				Salary			
Balance c/d				Profit share			
				Balance c/d			
	———	———	———		———	———	———
	———	———	———		———	———	———
Balance b/d				Balance b/d			

3.3   Changes in salary, interest and profit share

The partnership agreement may be changed during a period so that all three variables (salary, interest and profit share) are altered during the period.

The profit must be divided into the two periods (assuming that all the changes are effective from the same day in the period) and any changes put into the appropriate period.

Example

X, Y and Z are in partnership for the year ended 31 December 20X8.

At the start of the year they share profits in the ratio 2:2:1. The net profit for the year was £144,000.

At 1 January 20X8 the partners' capital was

	£
X	100,000
Y	50,000
Z	40,000

For the period to 31 May 20X8, the partners received interest at 3% on their capital at the beginning of the year.

For the remainder of the year they received interest at 4% on their capital at the beginning of the year.

For the period to 31 May 20X8 Z received a salary of £18,000 per annum. For the remainder of the year Z received no salary and the profit share was changed to 3:2:2.

During the year the partners each drew £2,000 per month in drawings.

Task 1

Complete the table showing the salary and interest received by the partners during the year for the two separate periods and in total.

	1 Jan 08 – 31 May 08 £	1 June 08 – 31 Dec 08 £	Total £

Task 2

Complete the table showing the appropriation account for the partnership for both periods down to the line for the 'profits available for distribution'.

	1 Jan 08 – 31 May 08 £	1 June 08 – 31 Dec 08 £	Total £
Net profit			
Salaries			
X			
Y			
Z			
Interest			
X			
Y			
Z			
Profits available for distribution			

Task 3

Complete the appropriation account showing the profit shares for the partners and the balance left for distribution if any.

Task 4

Explain how drawings are entered in the books of accounts.

Solution

Task 1

	1 Jan 08 – 31 May 08 £	1 June 08 – 31 Dec 08 £	Total £
Interest			
X	100,000 × 3% × 5/12 = 1,250	100,000 × 4% × 7/12 = 2,333	3,583
Y	50,000 × 3% × 5/12 = 625	50,000 × 4% × 7/12 = 1,167	1,792
Z	40,000 × 3% × 5/12 = 500	40,000 × 4% × 7/12 = 933	1,433

Task 2 and 3

Appropriation account for the year to 31 December 2008

	1 Jan 08 – 31 May 08 £	1 June 08 – 31 Dec 08 £	Total £
Net profit	**60,000**	**84,000**	**144,000**
Salaries			
X			
Y			
Z (18,000 × 5/12)	7,500		7,500
Interest			
X	1,250	2,333	3,583
Y	625	1,167	1,792
Z	500	933	1,433
Profit available for distribution	**50,125**	**79,567**	**129,692**
Profit share			
X	(50,125 × 2/5) 20,050	(79,567 × 3/7) 34,100	54,150
Y	(50,125 × 2/5) 20,050	(79,567 × 2/7) 22,733	42,783
Z	(50,125 × 1/5) 10,025	(79,567 × 2/7) 22,734	32,759
Balance	**Nil**	**Nil**	**Nil**

Task 4

Drawings are not an expense of the business or a form of remuneration for the partners.

They are simply the partners taking money out of the business on account of the profit share that they will eventually receive.

The drawings are therefore not entered in the partnership profit and loss account, but are entered as a debit in the partners' current accounts.

4 Admission of a new partner

4.1 Introduction

When a new partner is admitted to the partnership then the partners will agree a certain sum of cash that the new partner must pay for his share in the partnership. The basic double entry for the cash that the new partner brings into the partnership is:

Debit Bank account

Credit New partner's capital account

However, there is a complication in that we need to consider the goodwill of the partnership.

4.2   Goodwill

As well as the net assets that a partnership have recorded in their ledger accounts such as machinery, motor vehicles, debtors, stock, creditors, etc, most businesses will have another asset which is not recorded in the ledger accounts, being goodwill.

Goodwill comes about due to the excellence or reputation of the business. It can be due to good quality products, good after sales service, good location, excellence of employees and many other factors.

The problem with goodwill is that not only is it very difficult to measure in monetary terms but it is also very volatile.

Goodwill is essentially the value of the business as a whole over and above the value of the recorded net assets, unless the business is actually being sold then this total value is only an estimate.

A further problem is the nature of goodwill. Suppose that the goodwill of a restaurant business has been built up due to the reputation of the head chef then if that chef leaves or there is a bout of food poisoning in the restaurant, the goodwill is wiped out overnight.

Due to these problems, such goodwill is not recognised in the financial statements of a business. However, there is little doubt that it does exist in many businesses.

4.3   Goodwill and admission of a new partner

When a new partner is admitted to a partnership he will be buying not only a share of the recorded assets of the business but also a share of the unrecorded goodwill in the business.

This must be recognised in the accounting procedures.

Step 1

Immediately before the admission of the new partner, the amount of goodwill that the old partners have built up must be recognised and shared out between the partners. This is done by the following double entry:

Debit   Goodwill account with the estimated value of the goodwill

Credit   Old partners' capital accounts in the old profit share ratio

Step 2

The new partner will now be admitted and the cash that he brings into the partnership is accounted for by:

Debit   Bank account

Credit New partner's capital account

Step 3

Finally the goodwill must be eliminated from the books. This is done by:

Debit   New partners' capital accounts in the new profit share ratio

Credit Goodwill account with the value of the goodwill

By this stage the goodwill has been taken out of the accounts again and the partners' capital account balances have been adjusted to account for the old partners' share of the goodwill they have earned and the new partner's purchase of not only a share of the recorded net assets but also his share of the unrecorded asset goodwill.

 Example

Pete and Paul have been in partnership for a number of years sharing profits equally.

The balance on Pete's capital account is £100,000 and the balance on Paul's capital account is £80,000.

They have decided to admit a new partner to the partnership, Phil. Phil will contribute £60,000 in cash to the partnership on his admission and the profit share ratio after he is admitted will be two fifths of profits for Pete and Paul and one fifth of profits for Phil.

The goodwill in the partnership is estimated to be £30,000.

Write up the partners' capital accounts to reflect the admission of Phil.

Solution

Step 1

Set up the goodwill account (temporarily) and credit the old partners in the old profit share ratio in their capital accounts.

Goodwill account			
	£		£
Capital accounts	30,000		

Capital accounts

	Pete £	Paul £		Pete £	Paul £
			Balance b/d	100,000	80,000
			Goodwill	15,000	15,000

Step 2

Introduce the new partner and his capital

Capital accounts

	Pete £	Paul £	Phil £		Pete £	Paul £	Phil £
				Bal b/d	100,000	80,000	
				Goodwill	15,000	15,000	
				Bank			60,000

Step 3

Eliminate the goodwill by debiting all of the partners' capital accounts in the new profit share ratio and crediting the goodwill account.

Goodwill account

	£		£
Capital accounts	30,000	Capital accounts	30,000

Capital accounts

	Pete £	Paul £	Phil £		Pete £	Paul £	Phil £
Goodwill	12,000	12,000	6,000	Bal b/d	100,000	80,000	
				Goodwill	15,000	15,000	
Bal b/d	103,000	83,000	54,000	Bank			60,000
	115,000	95,000	60,000		115,000	95,000	60,000
				Bal b/d	103,000	83,000	54,000

What has happened here is that Phil has purchased with his £60,000 a share of the recorded net assets of the business for £54,000, his capital balance, but he has also purchased for £6,000 his share of the goodwill of the business which is unrecorded.

He has effectively purchased this from Pete and Paul for £3,000 each as their capital balances have increased by £3,000 in total each.

Activity 4

Karl and Len have been in partnership for a number of years sharing profits in the ratio of 2 : 1.

They have capital account balances of £80,000 and £50,000 respectively.

On 30 June 20X4 they have invited Nina to join the partnership and she is to introduce £35,000 of capital.

From this date the profits are to be shared with two fifths to Karl and Len and one fifth to Nina. The goodwill of the partnership at 30 June 20X4 is estimated to be £15,000.

Write up the partners' capital accounts to reflect the admission of Nina.

Capital accounts

	Karl £	Len £	Nina £		Karl £	Len £	Nina £
	___	___	___		___	___	___
	___	___	___		___	___	___

5 Retirement of a partner

5.1 Introduction

When a partner retires from a partnership the full amounts that are due to him must be calculated. This will include his capital account balance, his current account balance plus his share of any goodwill that the partnership has. The adjustments in the partners' capital accounts to reflect all of this are very similar to those for the admission of a new partner.

5.2 Accounting adjustments

On the retirement of a partner there are a number of accounting adjustments that must take place to ensure that the full amounts due to the retiring partner are paid to him.

Step 1

Transfer the retiring partner's current account balance to his capital account so that we are only dealing with one account.

Debit   Partners' current account balance

Credit Partners' capital account

Step 2

Recognise the goodwill that has been built up in the partnership by temporarily setting up a goodwill account and crediting all of the partners with their share of the goodwill.

Debit   Goodwill account with the value of the goodwill on the retirement date

Credit Partners' capital accounts in their profit sharing ratio

Step 3

Now the retiring partner has the total balance that is due to him in his capital account. He must then be paid off. The simplest method is to pay him what is due to him in cash:

Debit   Retiring partner's capital account with the balance due

Credit Bank account

The partnership may not have enough cash to pay off all that is due to the partner so, instead, the retiring partner leaves some or all of what is due to him as a loan to the partnership that will be repaid in the future.

Debit   Retiring partner's capital account

Credit Loan account

Step 4

We must now remove the goodwill from the ledger by:

Debit   Remaining partners' capital accounts in profit share ratio

Credit Goodwill account with the value of the goodwill

Example

Rob, Marc and Di have been in partnership for a number of years sharing profits in the ratio of 3 : 2 : 1.

On 1 March 20X3 Rob retired from the partnership and at that date the goodwill was valued at £60,000.

The other two partners agreed with Rob that he would be paid £20,000 of what was due to him in cash and the remainder would be a loan to the partnership.

After Rob's retirement Marc and Di are to share profits in the ratio of 2:1.

The capital account and current account balances at 1 March 20X3 were as follows:

		£
Capital accounts	– Rob	65,000
	Marc	55,000
	Di	40,000
Current accounts	– Rob	8,000
	Marc	5,000
	Di	2,000

Write up the partners' capital accounts to reflect the retirement of Rob.

Solution

Step 1

Transfer Rob's current account balance to his capital account.

Capital accounts

	Rob £	Marc £	Di £		Rob £	Marc £	Di £
				Bal b/d	65,000	55,000	40,000
				Current a/c	8,000		

Current accounts

	Rob £	Marc £	Di £		Rob £	Marc £	Di £
Capital a/c	8,000			Bal b/d	8,000	5,000	2,000

Step 2

Temporarily open up a goodwill account and credit the partners' capital accounts in the old profit sharing ratio.

Goodwill account

	£		£
Capital accounts	60,000		

Capital accounts

	Rob £	Marc £	Di £		Rob £	Marc £	Di £
				Bal b/d	65,000	55,000	40,000
				Current a/c	8,000		
				Goodwill	30,000	20,000	10,000

Step 3

Pay Rob off as agreed – £20,000 in cash and the remainder as a loan.

Capital accounts

	Rob £	Marc £	Di £		Rob £	Marc £	Di £
Bank	20,000			Bal b/d	65,000	55,000	40,000
Loan	83,000			Current a/c	8,000		
				Goodwill	30,000	20,000	10,000
	_____				_____		
	103,000				103,000		
	_____				_____		

Step 4

Remove the goodwill from the ledger with a credit to the goodwill account and a debit to the remaining partners' capital accounts in the new profit share ratio.

Goodwill account

	£		£
Capital accounts	60,000	Capital accounts	60,000
	_____		_____

Capital accounts

	Rob £	Marc £	Di £		Rob £	Marc £	Di £
Bank	20,000			Bal b/d	65,000	55,000	40,000
Loan	83,000			Current a/c	8,000		
Goodwill		40,000	20,000				
Bal c/d	—	35,000	30,000	Goodwill	30,000	20,000	10,000
	103,000	75,000	50,000		103,000	75,000	50,000
				Bal c/d		35,000	30,000

You can see that Marc's capital account balance has reduced by £20,000 and that Di's has reduced by £10,000.

They have effectively been charged with the £30,000 of goodwill that has to be paid to Rob on his retirement.

 Activity 5

M, N and P have been in partnership for a number of years sharing profits equally.

On 30 June 20X4 M is to retire from the partnership and thereafter N and P will share profits equally.

The value of the goodwill of the partnership is estimated to be £30,000 and M has agreed to leave the entire amount due to him on loan to the partnership.

The capital and current account balances at 30 June 20X4 are as follows:

Current accounts

	M £	N £	P £		M £	N £	P £
				Balance b/d	4,000	5,000	6,000

Write up the partners' capital accounts to reflect the retirement of M.

Capital accounts

	M £	N £	P £		M £	N £	P £
				Balance b/d	50,000	40,000	30,000
	___	___	___		___	___	___
	___	___	___		___	___	___

6 Preparing final accounts for a partnership

6.1   Profit and loss account

The first stage in preparing a partnership's final accounts from either a trial balance or an extended trial balance is to prepare the profit and loss account. This will be exactly the same as the preparation of a profit and loss account for a sole trader with the same types of adjustments such as depreciation expenses, closing stock, irrecoverable and doubtful debts and accruals and repayments

6.2   Appropriation of profit

The next stage is to take the net profit from the profit and loss account and prepare an appropriation account in order to split the profit between the partners in their current accounts according to the profit share ratio.

Remember that if the profit share ratio has changed during the period, the appropriation must be done in two separate calculations.

6.3   Drawings

In the trial balance there will be account balances for each partner's drawings, these must be transferred to the partners' current accounts and the balance on each partner's current account found.

6.4   Balance sheet

The final stage is to prepare the balance sheet of the partnership. The top part of the balance sheet will be exactly the same as that for a sole trader.

Only the capital section of the balance sheet is different. Here the capital account balances and the current account balances for each partner are listed and totalled, and this total should agree with the net assets total of the top part of the balance sheet.

 Example

A, B and C are in partnership with a partnership agreement that B receives a salary of £8,000 per annum and C a salary of £12,000 per annum.

Interest on capital is allowed at 4% per annum and the profits are shared in the ratio of 2 : 1 : 1.

The list of ledger balances at the year end of 31 March 20X4 are given below:

		£
Drawings	A	43,200
	B	26,000
	C	30,200
Purchases ledger control account		56,000
Bank balance		2,800
Current accounts at 1 April 20X3	A	3,500
	B	7,000
	C	4,200
Purchases		422,800
Stock at 1 April 20X3		63,000
Capital accounts	A	42,000
	B	32,200
	C	14,000
Sales ledger control account		75,600
Sales		651,000
Fixed assets at cost		112,000
Accumulated depreciation at 1 April 20X3		58,900
Allowance for doubtful debts at 1 April 20X3		2,000
Expenses		95,200

You are also given the following information:

(i)   Stock at 31 March 20X4 has been valued at £70,000.

(ii) Depreciation for the year has yet to be provided at 20% on cost.

(iii) An irrecoverable debt of £5,600 is to be written off and an allowance for doubtful debts is to be 2% of the remaining debtors.

(iv) Expenses of £7,000 are to be accrued.

Task 1

Draw up are initial trial balance at 31 March 20X4

Trial balance at 31 March 20X4

		£	£
Drawings	A	43,200	
	B	26,000	
	C	30,200	
Purchases ledger control account			56,000
Bank balance		2,800	
Current accounts at 1 April 20X3	A		3,500
	B		7,000
	C		4,200
Purchases		422,800	
Capital accounts	A		42,000
	B		32,200
	C		14,000
Stock at 1 April 20X3		63,000	
Sales ledger control account		75,600	
Sales			651,000
Fixed assets at cost		112,000	
Accumulated depreciation at 1 April 20X3			58,900
Allowance for doubtful debts at 1 April 20X3			2,000
Expenses		95,200	
		870,800	870,800

Task 2

Prepare the profit and loss account for the year ending 31 March 20X4.

Profit and loss account for the year ending 31 March 20X4

	£	£
Sales		651,000
Less: Cost of sales		
Opening stock	63,000	
Purchases	422,800	
	485,800	
Less: Closing stock	(70,000)	
		415,800
Gross profit		235,200

Less:	Expenses (95,200 + 7,000)	102,200
	Depreciation (20% × 112,000)	22,400
	Irrecoverable debts	5,600
	Allowance in doubtful debt adjustment	
	(2% × (75,600 − 5,600) − 2,000)	(600)

Total expenses	129,600
Net profit	105,600

Task 3

Prepare the appropriation account.

Appropriation account

			£	£
Net profit				105,600
Salaries	–	B	8,000	
		C	12,000	
				(20,000)
Interest on capital	–	A (42,000 × 4%)	1,680	
		B (32,200 × 4%)	1,288	
		C (14,000 × 4%)	560	
				(3,528)
Profit for profit share				82,072
A (82,072 × 2/4)			41,036	
B (82,072 × 1/4)			20,518	
C (82,072 × 1/4)			20,518	
				82,072

Task 4

Prepare the partners current account to include salaries, interest, profit share and drawings.

Current accounts

	A £	B £	C £		A £	B £	C £
Drawings	43,200	26,000	30,200	Balance b/d	3,500	7,000	4,200
				Salaries		8,000	12,000
				Interest on cap	1,680	1,288	560
Balance c/d	3,016	10,806	7,078	Profit share	41,036	20,518	20,518
	46,216	36,806	37,278		46,216	36,806	37,278
				Balance b/d	3,016	10,806	7,078

Task 5

Prepare the balance sheet for the partnership at 31 March 20X4

Balance sheet as at 31 March 20X4

	£	£	£
Fixed assets at cost			112,000
Accumulated depreciation (58,900 + 22,400)			(81,300)
Net book value			30,700
Current assets			
Stock		70,000	
Trade debtors	70,000		
Less: Allowance for doubtful debts	(1,400)		
		68,600	
Bank		2,800	
		141,400	
Current liabilities:			
Trade creditors	56,000		
Accruals	7,000		
		(63,000)	
Net current assets			78,400
Net assets			109,100

		£	£
Capital accounts	– A	42,000	
	B	32,200	
	C	14,000	
			88,200
Capital accounts	– A	3,016	
	B	10,806	
	C	7,078	
			20,900
			109,100

Activity 6

The partnership of Lyle and Tate has made a net profit of £58,000 for the year ending 30 June 20X3.

The partnership agreement is that Tate receives a salary of £8,000 per annum and that the profits are split in the ratio of 3 : 2.

The list of balance sheet balances at 30 June 20X3 are given below:

			£
Capital accounts	–	Lyle	75,000
		Tate	50,000
Current accounts at 1 July 20X2	–	Lyle	3,000
		Tate	2,000
Drawings	–	Lyle	28,000
		Tate	24,000
Fixed assets at cost			100,000
Accumulated depreciation at 30 June 20X3			30,000
Stock at 30 June 20X3			44,000
Trade debtors			38,000
Bank			10,000
Trade creditors			26,000

Prepare the appropriation account

Appropriation account		£	£
Net profit			
Salary – Tate			
		―――	
Profit available			
		―――	
Profit share –	Lyle		
	Tate		
		―――	
		―――	

Write up and balance the partners' current accounts.

Current accounts

	Lyle £	Tate £		Lyle £	Tate £
Drawings			Balance b/d		
Balance c/d			Appropriation a/c		
	_____	_____		_____	_____
	_____	_____		_____	_____
			Balance b/d		

Prepare the partnership balance sheet as at 30 June 20X3.

Balance sheet as at 30 June 20X3

	£	£
Fixed assets at cost		
Accumulated depreciation		
		_____
Current assets		
Stock		
Trade Debtors		
Bank		
	_____	
Less: Trade creditors		
Net current assets		
		_____
Net assets		
		_____
Capital accounts	Lyle	
	Tate	
		_____
Current accounts	Lyle	
	Tate	
	_____	
		_____

Partnership accounts will always appear in the AAT exam but you will never have to deal with a partnership with more than three partners.

Activity 7

1   Is the usual balance on a partner's current account a debit or a credit? (Tick)

Debit   ☐

Credit   ☐

2   What is the double entry required to transfer a partner's drawings from the drawings account to the current account? (complete the account name in the box)

Debit   _____

Credit   _____

3   What is the double entry for interest on a partner's capital?

Debit   _____

Credit   _____

4   What is the goodwill of a partnership?

_____

_____

_____

_____

5   Goodwill is normally recorded as an asset?

True   ☐

False   ☐

7 Summary

In this chapter we have dealt with all aspects of partnership accounts which are required for the exam. The AAT examination will always feature partnership accounting so this is an important area. In terms of preparing final accounts for a partnership, the preparation of the profit and loss account is exactly the same as that for a sole trader, therefore in this chapter we have concentrated on the areas of difference between a sole trader and a partnership.

When partners pay capital into the partnership this is recorded in the partner's individual capital account. The profit of the partnership must then be shared between the partners according to the partnership agreement. This may include salaries for some partners, interest on capital as well as the final profit share ratio. All aspects of sharing out the profit take place in the appropriation account which can take the form of a ledger account or a vertical statement. The appropriated profit is credited to the partners' current accounts and their current accounts are debited with their drawings for the period. The balances on the partners' capital accounts and current accounts are listed in the bottom part of the balance sheet and should be equal in total to the net assets total of the top part of the balance sheet.

You may also be required to deal with changes in the partnership. The most straightforward of these is a change in the profit share ratio during the period. This requires a separate appropriation for the period before the change according to the old profit share ratio and then for the period after the change using the new profit share ratio.

If a partner is admitted to the partnership or a partner retires then the goodwill of the partnership has to be considered. The goodwill is not recorded in the partnership books but upon a change, such as an admission or retirement, it must be brought into account to ensure that each partner is given full credit, not only for the recorded assets but also for the goodwill. The treatment is fundamentally the same for both an admission and a retirement. The goodwill account is temporarily set up as a debit (an asset) and the partners' capital accounts are credited in the old profit share ratio. The goodwill is then removed with a credit entry to the goodwill account and debits to the partners' capital accounts in the new profit share ratio.

Answers to chapter activities

Activity 1

Capital account – A

	£		£
Balance c/d	20,000	Balance b/d	15,000
		Bank	5,000
	20,000		20,000
		Balance b/d	20,000

Capital account – B

	£		£
Balance c/d	15,000	Balance b/d	15,000
	15,000		15,000
		Balance b/d	15,000

Current account – A

	£		£
Drawings	12,000	Balance b/d	4,000
Balance c/d	6,000	Profit	14,000
	18,000		18,000
		Balance b/d	6,000

Current account – B

	£		£
Drawings	13,000	Balance b/d	2,000
Balance c/d	3,000	Profit	14,000
	16,000		16,000
		Balance b/d	3,000

Trial balance extract

	Dr £	Cr £
Capital account – A		20,000
Capital account – B		15,000
Current account – A		6,000
Current account – B		3,000

Activity 2

Appropriation account

		£	£
Net profit			120,000
Salary – Ted		20,000	
Interest on capital –	Nick (6% × 150,000)	9,000	
	Ted (6% × 100,000)	6,000	
			(35,000)
Profit available			85,000
Profit share –	Nick (85,000 × 3/5)		51,000
	Ted (85,000 × 2/5)		34,000
			85,000

Current accounts

	Nick £	Ted £		Nick £	Ted £
Balance b/d		1,000	Balance b/d	3,000	
Drawings	56,000	59,000	Salary		20,000
			Interest on capital	9,000	6,000
Balance c/d	7,000		Profit share	51,000	34,000
	63,000	60,000		63,000	60,000
			Balance b/d		7,000

Activity 3

Appropriation account

1.7.X3 to 31.3.X4			£
Profit to 31 March 20X4 (100,000 × 9/12)			75,000

Profit share	–	Jill (75,000 × 2/5)	30,000	
		Jane (75,000 × 2/5)	30,000	
		Jan (75,000 × 1/5)	15,000	
				75,000

1.4.X4 – 30.6.X4			
Profit to 30 June 20X4 (100,000 x 3/12)			25,000
Salary	Jane (16,000 × 3/12)		(4,000)
Profit available			21,000

Profit share	–	Jill (21,000 × 1/3)	7,000	
		Jane (21,000 x 1/3)	7,000	
		Jan (21,000 x 1/3)	7,000	
				21,000

Current accounts

	Jill £	Jane £	Jan £		Jill £	Jane £	Jan £
Drawings	38,000	40,000	25,000	Balance b/d	3,000	2,000	1,000
				Profit share	30,000	30,000	15,000
				Salary		4,000	
Balance c/d	2,000	3,000		Profit share	7,000	7,000	7,000
				Balance c/d			2,000
	40,000	43,000	25,000		40,000	43,000	25,000
Balance b/d			2,000	Balance b/d	2,000	3,000	

Activity 4

Capital accounts

	Karl £	Len £	Nina £		Karl £	Len £	Nina £
				Balance b/d	80,000	50,000	
Goodwill	6,000	6,000	3,000	Goodwill	10,000	5,000	
Balance c/d	84,000	49,000	32,000	Bank			35,000
	90,000	55,000	35,000		90,000	55,000	35,000
				Balance b/d	84,000	49,000	32,000

Activity 5

Capital accounts

	M £	N £	P £		M £	N £	P £
Goodwill		15,000	15,000	Balance b/d	50,000	40,000	30,000
Loan	64,000			Current a/c	4,000		
Balance c/d		35,000	25,000	Goodwill	10,000	10,000	10,000
	64,000	50,000	40,000		64,000	50,000	40,000
				Balance b/d		35,000	25,000

Activity 6

Appropriation account

	£	£
Net profit		58,000
Salary – Tate		(8,000)
Profit available		50,000
Profit share – Lyle (50,000 × 3/5)	30,000	
Tate (50,000 × 2/5)	20,000	
		50,000

Current accounts

	Lyle £	Tate £		Lyle £	Tate £
Drawings	28,000	24,000	Balance b/d	3,000	2,000
Balance c/d	5,000	6,000	Appropriation a/c	30,000	28,000
	33,000	30,000		33,000	30,000
			Balance b/d	5,000	6,000

Balance sheet as at 30 June 20X3

	£	£
Fixed assets at cost		100,000
Accumulated depreciation		(30,000)
		70,000
Current assets:		
Stock	44,000	
Trade debtors	38,000	
Bank	10,000	
	92,000	
Less: Trade creditors	(26,000)	
Net current assets		66,000
Net assets		136,000
Capital accounts	– Lyle		75,000
	Tate		50,000
			125,000
Current accounts	– Lyle	5,000	
	Tate	6,000	
			11,000
			136,000

Activity 7

1   Credit balance

2   Debit   Partner's current account
     Credit   Partner's drawings account

3   Debit   Appropriation account
     Credit   Partners' current accounts

4   It is the excess of the value of the partnership as a whole over the value of its net assets.

5   No, it is not recorded as an asset – False

8 Test your knowledge

Workbook Activity 8

Low, High and Broad

Low, High and Broad are in partnership sharing profits and losses in the ratio 2:2:1 respectively. Interest is credited on partners' capital account balances at the rate of 5% per annum.

High is the firm's sales manager and for his specialised services he is to receive a salary of £800 per annum.

During the year ended 30 April 20X1 the net profit of the firm was £6,200 and the partners' drawings were as follows:

	£
Low	1,200
High	800
Broad	800

On 31 October 20X0 the firm agreed that Low should withdraw £1,000 from his capital account and that Broad should subscribe a similar amount to his capital account.

The credit balances on the partners' accounts at 1 May 20X0 were as follows:

	Capital accounts	Current accounts
	£	£
Low	8,000	640
High	7,000	560
Broad	6,000	480

Required:

(a) Prepare a profit and loss appropriation statement for the year ended 30 April 20X1.

(b) Prepare the partners' capital and current accounts for the year ended 30 April 20X1.

KAPLAN PUBLISHING

Workbook Activity 9

Curran and Edgar are in partnership as motor engineers.

The following figures were available after the preparation of the trial balance at 31 December 20X3.

Capital account (C)	£26,000
Capital account (E)	£20,000
Current account (C)	£6,100
Current account (E)	£5,200

Both current accounts showed credit balances

Drawings (C)	£16,250
Drawings (E)	£14,750

After the preparation of the profit and loss account, profit was determined as £42,100.

Profits are shared equally by the partners.

Task 1

Show the capital account for each partner updated to 1 January 20X4.

Task 2

Prepare the current account for each partner, balancing these off at the year end.

Workbook Activity 10

You work as an accounting technician for John Turford, the proprietor of Whitby Engineering Services.

John is currently considering expanding the business by forming a partnership with his cousin, James North, who has experience of the business service John provides.

He sends you a note stating that he understands how his capital account is updated each year to show the effect of drawings and profit; but would like to know how, if he forms the partnership, the capital account will appear in future on the balance sheet; and will the treatment of drawings and profit be any different?

Write a short note to John in reply to his comments.

Workbook Activity 11

Kate and Ed have been in partnership for a number of years sharing profits and losses equally.

On 1 March 20X3 it was decided to admit Rob to the partnership and he would introduce £30,000 of additional capital by payment into the partnership bank account.

Kate and Ed had capital balances on 1 March 20X3 of £50,000 and £40,000 respectively and the goodwill of the partnership was estimated to be £35,000.

After the admission of Rob, the partnership profits are to be shared with two fifths to Kate and Ed each and one fifth to Rob.

Write up the partners' capital accounts to reflect the admission of Rob.

 Workbook Activity 12

Liam, Sam and Fred have been in partnership for a number of years sharing profits in the ratio of 3 : 2 : 1.

On 31 May 20X4 Liam is to retire from the partnership. He is due to be paid £20,000 on that date and the remainder is to remain as a loan to the partnership.

After Liam's retirement Sam and Fred are to share profits equally. The goodwill of the partnership at 31 May 20X4 was estimated to total £18,000.

The partners' capital and current account balances at 31 May 20X4 were as follows:

	£
Capital accounts	
Liam	50,000
Sam	40,000
Fred	30,000
Current accounts	
Liam	4,000
Sam	2,000
Fred	3,000

You are to write up the partners' capital accounts to reflect the retirement of Liam.

Incomplete records

3

Introduction

The reconstruction of financial information from incomplete evidence is an important element of the Accounts Preparation II syllabus in the context of a sole trader or a partnership.

There are a variety of techniques that can be used to reconstruct financial information when full accounting records have not been kept.

These include reconstruction of net asset totals, reconstruction of cash, bank, debtor and creditor accounts and the use of mark-ups or margins in order to calculate missing accounting figures.

Each of these techniques will be considered in this chapter.

KNOWLEDGE
Acquired from Accounts preparation I
Identify reasons for closing off accounts and producing a trial balance (4.1)
Explain the process, and limitations, of preparing a set of final accounts from a trial balance (4.2)

CONTENTS

1   What are incomplete records?
2   The net assets approach
3   Cash and bank account
4   Sales ledger control account and purchase ledger control account
5   Margins and mark-ups
6   Mark-ups and margins and incomplete records
7   Examination style questions

SKILLS

Calculate accurately the opening and/or closing capital using incomplete information (1.1)

Calculate accurately the opening and/or closing cash/bank account balance (1.2)

Prepare sales and purchase ledger control accounts and use these to correctly calculate sales, purchases and bank figures (1.3)

Calculate accurately account balances using mark ups and margins (1.4)

Prepare accurately journal entries or ledger accounts to take account of (1.5)

Closing stock

Accruals and prepayments

Depreciation

Allowance for doubtful debts

Irrecoverable debts

The gain/loss on disposal of a fixed asset

Purchase of assets

Produce a trial balance from accounting information (2.1)

Prepare a profit and loss account (income statement) (2.2)

Prepare a balance sheet (statement of financial position) (2.3)

1 What are incomplete records?

1.1 Introduction

So far in this text we have been considering the accounting systems of sole traders and partnerships. They have all kept full accounting records consisting of primary records and a full set of ledger accounts, leading to a trial balance from which final accounts could be prepared.

In this chapter we will be considering businesses that do not keep full accounting records – incomplete records.

1.2 Limited records

Many businesses especially those of small sole traders or partnerships will only keep the bare minimum of accounting records. These may typically consist of:

- bank statements;
- files of invoices sent to customers probably marked off when paid;
- files of invoices received from suppliers marked off when paid;
- files of bills marked off when paid;
- till rolls;
- record of fixed assets owned.

From these records it will normally be possible to piece together the information required to prepare a profit and loss account and a balance sheet but a number of techniques are required. These will all be covered in this chapter.

1.3 Destroyed records

In some situations, particularly in examinations, either the whole, or part, of the accounting records has been destroyed by fire, flood, thieves or computer failure. It will then be necessary to try to piece together the picture of the business from the information that is available.

1.4 Missing figures

A further element of incomplete records is that a particular figure or balance may be missing. These will typically be stock that has been destroyed by fire or drawings that are unknown. Incomplete records techniques can be used to find the missing balance as a balancing figure.

1.5   Techniques

In order to deal with these situations a number of specific accounting techniques are required and these will be dealt with in this chapter. They are:

- the net assets approach;

- the cash and bank account;

- debtors and creditors control accounts;

- mark ups and margins.

2   The net assets approach

2.1   Introduction

The net assets approach is used in a particular type of incomplete records situation. This is where there are no detailed records of the transactions of the business during the accounting period. This may be due to the fact that they have been destroyed or that they were never kept in the first place. The only facts that can be determined are the net assets at the start of the year, the net assets at the end of the year and some details about the capital of the business.

2.2   The accounting equation

We have come across the accounting equation in earlier chapters when dealing with balance sheets.

The basic accounting equation is that:

Net assets   =   Capital

This can also be expanded to:

Increase in net assets   =   Capital introduced + profit – drawings

This is important – any increase in the net assets of the business must be due to the introduction of new capital and/or the making of profit less drawings.

2.3   Using the accounting equation

If the opening net assets of the business can be determined and also the closing net assets then the increase in net assets is the difference.

Therefore if any capital introduced is known and also any drawings made by the owner then the profit for the period can be deduced.

Alternatively if the profit and capital introduced are known then the drawings can be found as the balancing figure.

 Example

Archibald started a business on 1 January 20X1 with £2,000. On 31 December 20X1 the position of the business was as follows:

	£
It owned	
Freehold lock–up shop cost	4,000
Shop fixtures and equipment, cost	500
Stock of goods bought for resale, cost	10,300
Debts owing by customers	500
Cash in till	10
Cash at bank	150
It owed	
Mortgage on shop premises	3,000
Creditors for goods	7,000
Accrued mortgage interest	100

Archibald had drawn £500 for personal living expenses.

The shop fittings are to be depreciated by £50 and certain goods in stock which had cost £300 can be sold for only £50.

No records had been maintained throughout the year.

You are required to calculate the profit earned by Archibald's business in the year ended 31 December 20X1.

Solution

This sort of question is answered by calculating the net assets at the year-end as follows:

Net assets at 31 December 20X1

	Cost £	Depreciation £	£
Fixed assets			
Freehold shop	4,000	–	4,000
Fixtures and fittings	500	50	450
	4,500	50	4,450

Current assets

Stock at lower of cost and net realisable value (10,300 – 300 + 50)		10,050
Trade debtors		500
Cash and bank balances		160
		10,710

Current liabilities

Trade creditors	7,000		
Mortgage interest	100		
		(7,100)	
			3,610
			8,060
Mortgage			(3,000)
Net assets			5,060

The profit is now calculated from the accounting equation.

Change in net assets during the year = Profit plus capital introduced less drawings

£5,060 – 2,000   = Profit + Nil – 500

£3,060   = Profit – 500

Therefore, profit = £3,560

Archibald's balance sheet is made up of the above together with the bottom half which can be established after calculating the profit, i.e.

	£
Capital	2,000
Profit (balancing figure)	3,560
	5,560
Drawings	(500)
	5,060

As you can see, the 'incomplete records' part of the question is concerned with just one figure. The question is really about the preparation of the balance sheet.

Activity 1

The net assets of a business at the start of the year were £14,600. At the end of the year the net assets were £17,300. During the year the owner had paid in £2,000 of additional long term capital and withdrawn £10,000 from the business for living expenses.

What is the profit of the business?

3 Cash and bank account

3.1 Introduction

In this section we must be quite clear about the distinction between cash and bank accounts.

 Definition

Cash is the amount of notes and coins in a till or in the petty cash box.

 Definition

The bank account is the amount actually held in the current account or cheque account of the business.

If the opening and closing balances of cash and bank are known together with most of the movements in and out, then, if there is only one missing figure this can be found as the balancing figure.

3.2 Cash account

When dealing with incomplete records a cash account deals literally with cash either from the petty cash box or more usually from the till in a small retail business. If the opening balance and the closing balance of cash is known then provided there is only one missing figure this can be determined from the summarised cash account.

Example

Henry's sales are all for cash. During the year he:

- banked £50,000;

- paid wages of £5,000 out of the till; and

- paid expenses in cash of £10,000.

What were Henry's sales?

Solution

Working cash account

	£		£
Cash sales (bal fig)	65,000	Bankings	50,000
		Wages	5,000
		Expenses	10,000
	————		————
	65,000		65,000
	————		————

The rationale is that if £65,000 of cash was taken out of the till for various purposes then £65,000 must have come in.

 Activity 2

Henrietta runs a milliner's shop making all her sales for cash. You ascertain the following information:

	£
Cash in the till at the beginning of the year	50
Cash in the till at the end of the year	75
Bingo winnings put into the till	500
Bankings	15,000
Cash wages	1,000
Cash expenses	5,000

What were Henrietta's sales during the year?

Complete the ledger account below to establish the sales figure.

Working cash account

	£		£

3.3 Bank account

The same ideas can be applied to the bank account – if the opening and closing balances and all of the transactions except one are known then this missing figure can be found. In practice this may not be required though as bank statements should show all the necessary details.

Note that the double entry for bankings is

Dr **Bank account**

Cr **Cash account**

Example

Henry writes cheques only for his own use. He knows that his bankings were £50,000.

The opening and closing bank balances were £10,000 and £40,000 respectively. What were his drawings?

Solution

Working bank account

	£		£
Balance b/d	10,000	Drawings (bal fig)	20,000
Bankings	50,000	Balance c/d	40,000
	60,000		60,000
Balance b/d	40,000		

The bankings are the amount paid out of the till and into the bank account. Therefore they must be a debit entry in the bank account.

3.4 Combined cash and bank account

In examinations or simulations it is often easier to combine the cash and bank accounts into one ledger account with a column for cash and a column for bank.

In the case of Henry this would be written as:

	Cash £	Bank £		Cash £	Bank £
Working cash and bank account					
Balance b/d		10,000	Drawings (bal fig)		20,000
Bankings		50,000	Bankings	50,000	
Cash sales (bal fig)	65,000		Wages	5,000	
			Expenses	10,000	
			Balance c/d		40,000
	65,000	60,000		65,000	60,000

The key figure here is the bankings. If the bankings were paid into the bank account then they must have come out of the till or cash account.

In examinations you may only be given the bankings figure from the bank statement – this will show the amount paid into the bank account. You must then ensure that you make this entry not only as a debit in the bank column but also as a credit in the cash column.

4 Sales ledger control account and purchase ledger control account

4.1 Introduction

In many incomplete records situations you will find that the figures for sales and purchases are missing.

A technique for finding these missing figures is to recreate the debtors and creditors accounts in order to find the missing figures as balancing figures.

The sales ledger control account and the purchase ledger control account are used to find the missing figures.

4.2 Sales ledger control account

Firstly a reminder of what is likely to be in a sales ledger control account is below:

Sales ledger control account

	£		£
Opening balance	X	Receipts from customers	X
Sales	X	Sales returns	X
		Irrecoverable debts	X
		Discounts allowed	X
		Contra with PLCA	X
		Closing balance	X
	X		X

If the opening and closing debtors are known, together with the receipts from customers and details of any irrecoverable debts then the sales figure can be found as the balancing figure.

Example

A business has debtors at the start of the year of £4,220 and at the end of the year debtors of £4,870.

During the year customers paid a total of £156,350 and one debt of £1,000 that was irrecoverable.

What were the sales for the year?

Solution

Sales ledger control account

	£		£
Opening balance	4,220	Receipts from customers	156,350
		Irrecoverable debt written off	1,000
Sales (bal fig)	158,000	Closing balance	4,870
	162,220		162,220

The sales figure of £158,000 can be deduced from this account as the balancing figure.

4.3 Purchase ledger control account

The purchase ledger control account works in the same way as a potential working for finding the purchases figure.

Purchase ledger control account			
	£		£
Payments to suppliers	X	Opening balance	X
Discount received	X	Purchases	X
Purchase returns	X		
Contra with SLCA	X		
Closing balance	X		
	X		X

🔆 Example

Dominic paid his creditors £5,000 during a period.

At the beginning of the period he owed £1,500 and at the end he owed £750.

What were his purchases for the period?

Solution

Purchase ledger control account			
	£		£
Cash	5,000	Balance b/d	1,500
Balance c/d	750	Purchases (bal fig)	4,250
	5,750		5,750
		Balance b/d	750

4.4 Cash, bank, debtors and creditors

In many incomplete records questions you will need to combine the techniques learnt so far.

You may need to use the cash and bank account in order to determine the receipts from customers and then transfer this amount to the sales ledger control account in order to find the sales figure.

Example

Andrea does not keep a full set of accounting records but she has been able to provide you with some information about her opening and closing balances for the year ended 31 December 20X1.

	1 January 20X1 £	31 December 20X1 £
Stock	5,227	4,892
Trade debtors	6,387	7,221
Trade creditors	3,859	4,209
Bank	1,448	1,382
Cash	450	300

You have also been provided with a summary of Andrea's payments out of her bank account:

	£
Payments to trade creditors	48,906
Purchase of new car	12,000
Payment of expenses	14,559

Andrea also tells you that she has taken £100 per week out of the till in cash in order to meet her own expenses.

Calculate sales, purchases, cost of sales and gross profit for Andrea for the year ended 31 December 20X1.

Solution

Step 1

Open up ledger accounts for cash and bank, debtors and creditors and enter the opening and closing balances given.

Cash and bank

	£	£		£	£
Opening balance	450	1,448	Closing balance	300	1,382

Sales ledger control account

	£		£
Opening balance	6,387	Closing balance	7,221

Purchase ledger control account

	£		£
Closing balance	4,209	Opening balance	3,859

Step 2

Enter the payments from the bank account in the credit column of the bank account and complete the double entry for the creditor's payment.

Cash and bank

	Cash £	Bank £		Cash £	Bank £
Opening balance	450	1,448	Creditors		48,906
			Car		12,000
			Expenses		14,559
			Closing balance	300	1,382

Purchase ledger control account

	£		£
Bank	48,906	Opening balance	3,859
Closing balance	4,209		

Step 3

Find the balancing figure in the bank account as this is the amount of money paid into the bank in the period. If it was paid into the bank it must have come out of the till therefore enter the same figure as a credit in the cash account.

Cash and bank

	Cash	Bank		Cash	Bank
Opening balance	450	1,448	Creditors		48,906
Bankings (bal fig)		75,399	Car		12,000
			Expenses		14,559
			Bankings	75,399	
			Closing balance	300	1,382
		———			———
		76,847			76,847
		———			———

Step 4

Enter the drawings into the cash account (assume a 52-week year unless told otherwise).

Cash and bank

	Cash £	Bank £		Cash £	Bank £
Opening balance	450	1,448	Creditors		48,906
Bankings (bal fig)		75,399	Car		12,000
			Expenses		14,559
			Bankings	75,399	
			Drawings	5,200	
			Closing balance	300	1,382
		———			———
		76,847			76,847
		———			———

Step 5

Balance the cash account – the missing figure is the amount of receipts from customers – this is a debit in the cash account and a credit in the Sales ledger control account.

Cash and bank

	Cash £	Bank £		Cash £	Bank £
Opening balance	450	1,448	Creditors		48,906
Bankings (bal fig)		75,399	Car		12,000
			Expenses		14,559
			Bankings	75,399	
			Drawings	5,200	
Receipts – debtors (bal fig)	80,449		Closing balance	300	1,382
	———	———		———	———
	80,899	76,847		80,899	76,847
	———	———		———	———

Sales ledger control account

	£		£
Opening balance	6,387	Receipts from customers	80,449
		Closing balance	7,221

The receipts figure of £80,449 is not technically all from debtors since some may be for cash sales; however as the Sales ledger control account is only a working account designed to find the total sales this distinction is unimportant.

Step 6

Find the sales and purchases figures as the missing figures in the debtors and creditors account.

Sales ledger control account

	£		£
Opening balance	6,387	Receipts from customers	80,449
Sales (bal fig)	81,283	Closing balance	7,221
	87,670		87,670

Purchase ledger control account

	£		£
Bank	48,906	Opening balance	3,859
Closing balance	4,209	Purchases (bal fig)	49,256
	53,115		53,115

Step 7

Prepare the Trading account

	£	£
Sales		81,283
Less: cost of sales		
Opening stock	5,227	
Purchases	49,256	
	54,483	
Less: closing stock	(4,892)	
		(49,591)
Gross profit		31,692

In this example we dealt with all four accounts – cash, bank, debtors and creditors- simultaneously in order to show how the double entry works between the four working accounts.

However in examinations you will be prompted to work through the situation step by step. So, this same example might be approached in the examination as follows:

Task 1

Calculate the amount of cash received from customers from sales.

This will come from the cash and bank account workings. Cash and bank.

Cash and bank

	Cash £	Bank £		Cash £	Bank £
Opening balance	450	1,448	Creditors		48,906
Bankings (bal fig)		75,399	Car		12,000
			Expenses		14,559
			Bankings	75,399	
			Drawings	5,200	
Receipts – debtors (bal fig)	80,449		Closing balance	300	1,382
	80,899	76,847		80,899	76,847

Cash from customers for sales = £80,449

Task 2

Determine the sales for the period.

This will come from the working Sales ledger control account.

Sales ledger control account

	£		£
Opening balance	6,387	Receipts from customers	80,449
Sales (bal fig)	81,283	Closing balance	7,221
	87,670		87,670

Sales = £81,283

Task 3

Determine the purchases for the period.

This will come from the working purchase ledger control account.

Purchase ledger control account

	£		£
Bank	48,906	Opening balance	3,859
Closing balance	4,209	Purchases (bal fig)	49,256
	53,115		53,115

Purchases = £49,256

Task 4

Calculate the gross profit for the period.

This will come from the working trading account.

	£	£
Sales		81,283
Less: cost of sales		
Opening stock	5,227	
Purchases	49,256	
	54,483	
Less: closing stock	(4,892)	
		(49,591)
Gross profit		31,692

Gross profit = £31,692

5 Margins and mark-ups

5.1 Introduction

The final technique that you may be required to use is that of dealing with margins and mark-ups. This is often useful when dealing with the records of a retailer and is a useful method of reconstructing missing figures.

5.2   Cost structure

The key to dealing with mark-ups and margins is in setting up the cost structure of the sales of an organisation from the information given in the question.

Definition

A cost structure is the relationship between the selling price of goods, their cost and the gross profit earned in percentage terms.

Example

An item is sold for £150 and it originally cost £100. We need to set up the cost structure for this sale.

Solution

	£
Sales	150
Cost of sales	100
Gross profit	50

The cost structure, in percentage terms, can be set up in one of two ways.

(i)   Assume that cost of sales represents 100% therefore the cost structure would be:

	£	%
Sales	150	150
Cost of sales	100	100
Gross profit	50	50

We can now say that this sale gives a gross profit percentage of 50% on cost of sales.

(ii) Assume that sales represents 100% therefore the cost structure would be:

	£	%
Sales	150	100
Cost of sales	100	$66^2/_3$
Gross profit	50	$33^1/_3$

We can now say that this sale gives a gross profit percentage of $33^1/_3$% on sales.

5.3 The difference between a mark-up and a margin

If it is cost of sales that is 100% then this is known as a mark-up. Therefore in the previous example the sale would be described as having a mark-up on cost of 50%.

If it is sales that is 100% then this is known as a margin. In the previous example the sale would be described as having a gross profit margin of $33^1/_3$%.

 Example

Calculate the cost of goods which have been sold for £1,200 on which a gross profit margin of 25% has been achieved.

Solution

Step 1

Work out the cost structure.

The phrase 'gross profit margin' means 'gross profit on sales'. Following the rule above we therefore make sales equal to 100%. We know the gross profit is 25%; therefore the cost of sales must be 75%.

	%
Sales	100
Less: cost of sales	75
Gross profit	25

Step 2

Work out the missing figure, in this case 'cost of sales'.

	£	%
Sales	1,200	100
Cost of sales	?	75
Gross profit	?	25

Cost of goods sold = 75% of sales

$$= \frac{75}{100} \times 1,200 = £900$$

Therefore gross profit = £300 (£1,200 - £900)

 Example

Calculate the cost of goods which have been sold for £1,200 on which a mark-up on cost of sales of 25% has been achieved.

Solution

Step 1

The cost structure

The fact that the gross profit here is on cost of sales rather than sales as above makes all the difference. When we construct the 'cost structure', cost of sales will be 100%; gross profit will be 25%, so that sales must be 125%.

In other words:

	%
Sales	125
Less: cost of sales	100
Gross profit	25

Step 2

Calculate the missing figure, again the cost of sales

	£	%
Sales	1,200	125
Cost of sales	?	100
Gross profit	?	25

Cost of goods sold = $\dfrac{100}{125}$ of sales

$= \dfrac{100}{125} \times 1{,}200 = £960$

Remember the rule – whatever the margin or mark-up is 'on' or 'of' must be 100%.

• If there is a margin on sales price then sales are 100%.

• If there is a mark-up on cost then cost of sales are 100%.

Activity 3

(a) Mark-up on cost of sales = 10%
Sales were £6,160
Cost of sales =

(b) Gross profit on sales = 20%
Cost of sales was £20,000
Sales =

(c) Mark-up on cost of sales = 33%
Cost of sales was £15,000
Sales =

(d) Gross profit on sales = 25%
Cost of sales was £13,200
Sales =

(e) Sales were £20,000
Cost of sales was £16,000
Gross profit on sales as a % =
and on cost of sales as a % =

6 Mark-ups and margins and incomplete records

6.1 Introduction

We will now look at how mark-ups and margins can be used in incomplete records questions. They can be a great help in finding missing sales and cost of sales figures but a little practice is required in using them.

6.2 Calculating sales

In a question if you have enough information to calculate cost of sales and you are given some information about the cost structure of the sales then you will be able to calculate sales.

In examination questions if the percentage mark-up or margin is given then you will need to use it – do not try to answer the question without using it as you will get the answer wrong!

 Example

A business has purchases of £18,000 and opening and closing stock of £2,000 and £4,000 respectively. The gross profit margin is always 25%.

What are the sales for the period?

Solution

Step 1

Cost structure

As it is a gross profit margin this is a margin 'on' sales and therefore sales are 100%

	%
Sales	100
Cost of sales	75
	___
Gross profit	25
	___

Step 2

Calculate cost of sales

	£
Opening stock	2,000
Purchases	18,000
	20,000
Less: closing stock	(4,000)
	16,000

Step 3

Determine the sales figure

$$£16,000 \times \frac{100}{75} = £21,333$$

Activity 4

You are given the following information relating to Clarence's business for the year ended 31 December 20X3.

Cash paid to trade creditors £9,000. Other assets and liabilities:

	1 January	31 December
	£	£
Creditors	2,100	2,600
Stock	1,800	1,600

Mark-up on cost of sales 20%

Task 1

Calculate the purchases for the year.

Task 2

Calculate the cost of sales for the year.

Task 3

Calculate the sales for the year.

6.3 Calculating cost of sales, purchases or closing stock

If you know the figure for sales and you know about the cost structure then it is possible to find the total for cost of sales and then deduce any missing figures such as purchases or closing stock.

Example

A business had made sales in the month of £25,000. The business sells its goods at a mark-up of 20%.

The opening stock was £2,000 and the closing stock was £3,000.

What were the purchases for the period?

Solution

Step 1

Cost structure

	%
Sales	120
Cost of sales	100

Gross profit	20

Step 2

Determine cost of sales using the cost structure.

$$\text{Cost of sales} = £25,000 \times \frac{100}{120}$$

$$= £20,833$$

Step 3

Reconstruct cost of sales to find purchases

	£
Opening stock	2,000
Purchases (bal fig)	21,833

	23,833
Less: closing stock	(3,000)

Cost of sales	20,833
	---

7 Examination style questions

7.1 Introduction

So far we have studied the techniques that you have to use to deal with incomplete records questions in the exam. Although the examiner may ask any style of question, the examiner tends to ask questions in a particular way – leading you through the question a bit at a time and telling you what you have to calculate next. We shall now see how these questions might appear in the exam.

 Example

John is a sole trader and prepares his accounts to 30 September 20X8. The summary of his bank account is as follows.

	£		£
Balance b/d 1 Oct 20X7	15,000	Stationery	2,400
Receipts from debtors	74,865	General expenses	4,300
		Rent	4,500
		Creditors for purchases	27,000
		Drawings	24,000
		Balance at 30 Sept 20X8	27,665
	89,865		**89,865**

Debtors at 1 October 20X7 were 24,000 and at 30 September 20X8 were 30,000.

Creditors at 1 October 20X7 were 17,500 and at 30 September 20X8 were 23,000.

Rent was paid at £1,500 per quarter, and the rent had not been paid for the final quarter to 30 September 20X8.

During September 20X8 a payment of £300 was made for electricity which covered the period 1 August 20X8 to 31 October 20X8. Electricity is included in general expenses.

Task 1

Calculate the capital at 1 October 20X7.

Task 2

Prepare the sales ledger control account for the year ended 30 September 20X8, showing credit sales as the balancing figure.

Sales ledger control account

	£		£

Task 3

Prepare the purchases ledger control account for the year ended 30 September 20X8, showing credit purchases as the balancing figure.

Purchases ledger control account

	£		£

Task 4

Prepare the rent account for the year ended 30 September 20X8.

Rent account

	£		£

Task 5

Prepare the electricity account for the year ended 30 September 20X8.

General expenses account

	£		£

Task 6

Prepare a trial balance at 30 September 20X8

Solution

Task 1

Capital at 1 October 20X7

	£
Bank	15,000
Debtors	24,000
Creditors	(17,500)
Capital	21,500

Tutorial note. Remember that capital equals net assets. You therefore have to list all the assets and liabilities at the start of the year to find the net assets and therefore the capital.

Task 2

Sales ledger control account

	£		£
Balance b/d 1 Oct 20X7	24,000	Cash from debtors	74,865
Credit sales (bal fig)	80,865	Balance c/d 30 Sept 20X8	30,000
	104,865		104,865

Task 3

Purchases ledger control account

	£		£
Paid to creditors	27,000	Balance b/d 1 Oct 20X7	17,500
Balance c/d 30 Sept 20X8	23,000	Purchases (bal fig)	32,500
	———		———
	50,000		50,000
	———		———

Task 4

Rent account

	£		£
Cash paid	4,500	P and L a/c	6,000
Balance c/d	1,500		
	———		———
	6,000		6,000
	———		———

Tutorial note. The £1,500 rent that has not been paid for the final quarter is an accrual – it is brought down into the next period as a credit balance as it is money owed by the business.

Task 5

General expenses account

	£		£
Cash paid	4,300	P and L a/c	4,200
		Balance c/d (1/3 × £300)	100
	———		———
	4,300		4,300
	———		———

Tutorial note. Of the £300 paid in September 20X8, £100 is for the month of October 20X8 – it is therefore a prepayment and is carried forward as an asset – a debit balance

Task 6

Trial balance as at 30 September 20X8

	£	£
Capital at 1 October 20X7		21,500
Bank	27,665	
Sales		80,865
Sales ledger control a/c	30,000	
Purchases	32,500	
Purchases ledger control a/c		23,000
Accrual – rent		1,500
Prepayment – general expenses	100	
Stationery	2,400	
Rent (P and L a/c)	6,000	
General expenses (P and L a/c)	4,200	
Drawings	24,000	
	126,865	126,865

Tutorial note. This is a slightly unusual trial balance as it shows the expenses transferred to the Profit and Loss account as debit balances as well as all the normal credit and debit balances for the assets and liabilities at 30 September 20X8. This however is how the examiner may set the question and you must be ready for it.

7.2   Another example

In many examination questions you will be required to use the incomplete records techniques to determine missing figures. We have already looked at finding sales, cost of sales, purchases and closing or opening stock. The final common missing figure is that of the owner's drawings.

Often the owner of a business will not keep a record of exactly how much has been taken out of the business especially if money tends to be taken directly from the till.

In examination questions if you are told that the owner's drawings were approximately £35 each week then this figure can be used as the actual drawings figure.

However if the question states that drawings were between £25 and £45 per week you cannot take an average figure; you must use incomplete records techniques to find the drawings figure as the balancing figure.

Example

Simone runs a television and video shop.

All purchases are made on credit.

Sales are a mixture of cash and credit.

For the year ended 31 December 20X8, the opening and closing creditors, debtors and stocks were:

	1.1.X8 £	21.12.X8 £
Creditors	11,000	11,500
Debtors	12,000	11,800
Stock	7,000	10,000

Her mark-up is 20% on cost.

A summary of her business's bank account for the year ended 31 December 20X8 is as follows. The payments for purchases are posted to the bank account and the purchase ledger control account.

All cash and cheques are posted to the cash account and Sales ledger control account. Surplus cash and cheques are then paid into the bank.

Bank account

	£		£
Balance b/d 1/1/X8	12,500	Suppliers for purchases	114,000
Cash and cheques banked	121,000	Rent and rates	10,000
		Other expenses	4,000
		Balance c/d 31.12.X8	5,500
	133,500		133,500

The opening and closing cash balances were:

1/1/X8	31.12.X8
£120	£150

Simone made the following payments out of the till during the year:

	£
Petrol	400
Stationery	200

She also drew money out of the till for her personal use, but she has not kept a record of the amounts drawn.

Task 1

Prepare the purchase ledger control account

	£		£

Task 2

Calculate the cost of sales using the following proforma

                                                                                £

Opening stock

Purchases

                                                                         _____

Closing stock

                                                                         _____

Cost of sales

                                                                         _____

Task 3

Calculate the sales for the year using the following proforma and the details of the mark up given in the question.

                                                            £   %

Sales

Cost of sales

                                                   _____

Gross profit

                                                   _____

Task 4

Prepare the Sales ledger control account

	£		£

Task 5

Complete the cash account given below where drawings will be the balancing figure

Cash account

	£		£
Balance b/d		Petrol	
Receipts – debtors		Stationery	
		Bankings – to bank a/c	
		Drawings	
		Balance c/d	

Solution

Task 1

Calculation of purchases

Purchase ledger control account

	£		£
Bank account	114,000	Balance b/d	11,000
Balance c/d	11,500	Purchases (bal fig)	114,500
	125,500		125,500

Task 2

Calculation of cost of sales

	£
Opening stock	7,000
Purchases (Task 1)	114,500
	121,500
Closing stock	(10,000)
	111,500

Task 3

Calculation of sales

	£	%
Sales ($\frac{120}{100}$ × 111,500)	133,800	120
Cost of sales (Task 2)	111,500	100
Gross profit	22,300	20

Task 4

Sales ledger control account

	£		£
Balance b/d	12,000	Receipts (bal fig)	134,000
Sales (Task 3)	133,800	Balance c/d	11,800
	145,800		145,800

Task 5

Drawings

Cash account

	£		£
Balance b/d	120	Petrol	400
Receipts – debtors	134,000	Stationery	200
		Bankings	121,000
		Drawings (bal fig)	12,370
		Balance c/d	150
	134,120		134,120

Take care with the order in which you work.

- As a mark-up is given you will need to use it – you have enough information to determine purchases and cost of sales therefore use the mark-up to calculate sales.

- Make sure that you enter these sales into the Sales ledger control account on the debit side – even though some are for cash rather than on credit they should all be entered into the debtors account as you are only using it as a vehicle for calculating the total sales.

- Once sales have been entered into the debtors account the only missing figure is the cash received – this should be then entered into the cash account as a debit.

- Finally once all of the cash payments are entered as credits the balancing figure on the credit side of the cash account will be the drawings.

 Activity 5

Ignatius owns a small wholesale business and has come to you for assistance in the preparation of his accounts for the year ended 31 December 20X4.

For the year ended 31 December 20X4 no proper accounting records have been kept, but you establish the following information:

(1) A summary of Ignatius's bank statements for the year to 31 December 20X4 is as follows:

	£		£
Opening balance	1,870	Payments to suppliers	59,660
Receipts from credit customers	12,525	Rent – one year	4,000
Cash banked	59,000	Rates – year beginning 1.4.X4	2,000
		Other administration costs	1,335
		Selling costs	1,940
		Equipment – bought 1.1.X4	800
			69,735
		Closing balance	3,660
	73,395		73,395

(2) Credit sales for the year, as shown by a summary of copy invoices, totalled £12,760.

---

(3) No record has been kept by Ignatius of cash sales or his personal drawings, in cash. It is apparent, however, that all sales are on the basis of a $33\frac{1}{3}\%$ mark-up on cost.

(4) Apart from drawings, cash payments during the year have been:

	£
Payments to suppliers	755
Sundry expenses	155
Wages	3,055

The balance of cash in hand at 31 December 20X4 is estimated at £20, and it is known that £12 was in hand at the beginning of the year.

(5) At the year-end, closing stock, valued at cost, was £5,375 (31 December 20X3 £4,570) and creditors for goods bought for resale amounted to £4,655.

(6) At 31 December 20X3 creditors for goods bought for resale amounted to 3,845.

Task 1

Calculate the purchases for the year

Purchase ledger control account

	£		£
	_____		_____
	_____		_____

Task 2

Calculate the cost of sales for the year

	£
Opening stock 1.1.X4	
Purchases	
	_____
Stock 31.12.X4	
	_____
Cost of sales	
	_____

Task 3

Calculate the total sales for the year

Sales = (workings)

Cost structure

Cost of sales   =

Mark-up   =

Therefore sales   =

Task 4

Calculate the cash sales for the year

£

_____

Cash sales

_____

Task 5

Prepare calculations to determine the owner's drawings for the year.

Enter the cash sales in the cash account. This will give drawings as a balancing figure. The cash account is reproduced here.

Cash account			
£			£
_____			_____
_____			_____

Activity 6

1   According to the accounting equation, what is an increase in net assets equal to? (Write your answer below.)

2   What is the double entry for cash takings paid into the bank account? (Circle as appropriate.)

Debit   **Sales account / Bank account**

Credit   **Cash account / Takings account**

3   The opening and closing debtors for a business were £1,000 and £1,500 and receipts from customers totalled £17,500. What were sales? (Circle as appropriate.)

Sales are: **£17,500 / £17,000 / £18,000**

4   The opening and closing creditors for a business were £800 and £1,200 with payments to suppliers totalling £12,200. What is the purchases figure? (Circle as appropriate.)

Purchases are: **£12,600 / £12,200 / £11,800**

5   Goods costing £2,000 were sold at a mark up of 20%. What was the selling price? (Circle as appropriate.)

Selling price is: **£2,500 / £2,400**

6   Goods costing £2,000 were sold with a margin of 20%. What was the selling price? (Circle as appropriate.)

Selling price is: **£2,500 / £2,400**

7   Sales were £24,000 and were at a margin of 25%. What is the figure for cost of sales? (Circle as appropriate.)

Cost of sales is: **£18,000 / £6,000**

8   Sales were £24,000 and were at a mark up of 25%. What is the figure for cost of sales? (Circle as appropriate.)

Cost of sales is   **£18,000 / £19,200**

9   Sales for a business were £100,000 achieved at a margin of 40%. Opening stock was £7,000 and purchases were £58,000. What is the figure for closing stock? (Complete the proforma.)

	£	£
Sales		
Less cost of goods sold		
Opening stock		
Purchases		
Less closing stock		
Gross profit		

10   Sales for a business were £80,000 and they were sold at a mark up of 25%. Opening and closing stocks were £10,000 and £8,000. What is the purchase total? (Complete the pro forma.)

	£	£
Sales		
Less cost of goods sold		
Opening stock		
Purchases		
Less closing stock		
Gross profit		

8 Summary

This chapter has covered all of the varying techniques that might be required to deal with an incomplete records problem in an examination.

The techniques are the net assets approach, cash and bank accounts, Sales ledger control account and purchase ledger control account accounts and mark-ups and margins.

Many of these questions will look formidable in an examination but they are all answerable if you think about all of these techniques that you have learnt and apply them to the particular circumstances of the question.

You will also find that the AAT style is to lead you through a question with small tasks prompting you to carry out the calculations in a particular order which makes the process more manageable.

Answers to chapter activities

Activity 1

Increase in net assets	=	capital introduced	+ profit – drawings
(17,300 – 14,600)	=	2,000	+ profit – 10,000
2,700	=	2,000	+ profit – 10,000
Profit	=	£10,700	

Activity 2

Working cash account

	£		£
Balance b/d	50	Bankings	15,000
Capital (Bingo)	500	Wages	1,000
Cash sales (bal fig)	20,525	Expenses	5,000
		Balance c/d	75
	21,075		21,075

The rationale is that £21,075 has been 'used' for bankings, expenses and providing a float to start the next period therefore £21,075 must have been received.

Of this 'receipt':

- £50 is from last period; and

- £500 is an injection of capital.

Therefore £20,525 must have been sales.

Activity 3

		%	£
(a)	Cost of sales	100	
	Add: Mark–up	10	
	Therefore sales	110	
	Therefore cost of sales	$^{100}/_{110}$ × £6,160	5,600
(b)	Sales	100	
	Less: Gross profit	20	
	Therefore cost of sales	80	
	Therefore sales	$^{100}/_{80}$ × £20,000	25,000
(c)	Cost of sales	100	
	Add: Mark–up	33	
	Therefore sales	133	
	Therefore sales	$^{133}/_{100}$ × £15,000	19,950
(d)	Sales	100	
	Less: Gross profit	25	
	Therefore cost of sales	75	
	Therefore sales	$^{100}/_{75}$ × £13,200	17,600
(e)	Sales	20,000	
	Less: Cost of sales	16,000	
	Therefore gross profit	4,000	

Gross profit on sales $\dfrac{4,000}{20,000} \times \dfrac{100}{1} = 20\%$

Gross profit on cost of sales $\dfrac{4,000}{16,000} \times \dfrac{100}{1} = 25\%$

Activity 4

Task 1

Calculate the figure for purchases.

Purchase ledger control account

	£		£
Cash	9,000	Balance b/d	2,100
Balance c/d	2,600	Purchases (bal fig)	9,500
	11,600		11,600

Note that we are constructing the total account, and producing the balancing figure which represents the purchases made during the year.

Remember the double-entry involved here. The cash of £9,000 will be a credit in the cash account. The purchases (£9,500) will be debited to the purchases account and transferred to the trading and profit and loss account at the year-end:

Purchases account

	£		£
Purchase ledger control account	9,500	Trading profit and loss a/c	9,500

Task 2

Now complete the cost of sales

	£
Opening stock	1,800
Purchases	9,500
	11,300
Less: Closing stock	(1,600)
Cost of sales	9,700

Task 3

Now you can work out the cost structure and sales.

(a)   Work out the cost structure.

The mark-up is arrived at by reference to the cost of sales. Thus, cost of sales is 100%, the mark-up is 20% and therefore the sales are 120%:

	%
Sales (balancing figure)	120
Less: Gross profit	20
Cost of sales	100

(b)   Sales $= \dfrac{120}{100} \times$ cost of sales

$= \dfrac{120}{100} \times £9{,}700$

$= £11{,}640$

Activity 5

Task 1

Calculate purchases

Purchase ledger control account

	£		£
Cash – payments to suppliers	755	Creditors 1/1/X4	3,845
Bank – payments to suppliers	59,660	Purchases (balancing figure)	61,225
Creditors 31.12.X4	4,655		
	65,070		65,070

Task 2

Calculate the cost of sales.

	£
Opening stock 1.1.X4	4,570
Purchases	61,225
	65,795
Stock 31.12.X4	(5,375)
Cost of sales	60,420

Task 3

Calculate total sales

Cost of structure

Cost of sales	=	100%
Mark-up	=	$33^1/_3\%$
Therefore sales	=	$133^1/_3\%$

$$\text{Sales} = \frac{\text{Cost of sales}}{100} \times 133^1/_3\% = \frac{60,420}{100} \times 133^1/_3\% = £80,560$$

Task 4

Calculate cash sales

	£
Credit sales (per question)	12,760
Total sales	80,560
Therefore, cash sales	67,800

Task 5

Calculate drawings

Enter the cash sales in the cash account. This will give drawings as a balancing figure.

The cash account is reproduced here.

Cash account

	£		£
Balance 1.1.X4	12	Payments to suppliers	755
Receipts from cash sales	67,800	Other costs	155
		Wages	3,055
		Cash banked	59,000
		Drawings (balancing figure)	4,827
		Balance c/d	20
	_____		_____
	67,812		67,812
	_____		_____

Activity 6

1. Increase in net assets = capital introduced + profit – drawings

2. Debit   Bank account
   Credit   Cash account

3. £17,500 + 1,500 – £1,000   =   £18,000

4. £12,200 + £1,200 – £800   =   £12,600

5. £2,000 × 120/100   =   £2,400

6. £2,000 × 100/80   =   £2,500

7. £24,000 × 75/100   =   £18,000

8. £24,000 × 100/125   =   £19,200

9. Cost of sales = £100,000 × 60/100   =   £60,000
   Opening stock + purchases   =   £65,000
   Closing stock   =   £5,000

10. Cost of sales = £80,000 × 100/125   =   £64,000
    Purchases = £64,000 + £8,000 – £10,000   =   £62,000

9 Test your knowledge

Workbook Activity 7

You work as a senior for a self-employed 'Licensed Accounting Technician' and Peter Ryan, the proprietor of a local shop trading in 'home brew products', is one of your clients.

The business trades under the name of Brew-By-Us.

The balance sheet of the business at 31 May 20X0 was:

	Cost £	Depreciation £	NBV £
Fixed assets			
Shop lease	10,000	2,000	8,000
Fixtures and fittings	3,000	1,200	1,800
	13,000	3,200	9,800
Current assets			
Stock		3,500	
Rent and rates prepaid		950	
		4,450	
Less current liabilities			
Trade creditors		1,200	
Heat and light accrued		200	
Bank overdraft		750	
		2,150	
Net current assets			2,300
Net assets			12,100
Financed by			
Capital			12,100

All the business's sales are on a cash basis, and during the current year all the takings other than £10,400, used by Peter for his own personal needs, have been banked.

All payments for expenses have been made by cheque.

A summary of the bank transactions for the year ended 31 May 20X1 is as follows:

	£
Balance b/d	(750) overdrawn
Receipts	
Shop takings	49,560
	48,810
Payments	
Wages	3,850
Advertising	750
Payments to suppliers	36,200
Heat and light	1,060
Shop fixtures	2,000
Insurance	400
Rent and rates	5,400
Shop repairs	200
Bank charges and interest	320
	50,180
Balance 31 May 20X1	(1,370) overdrawn

Additional information for the year ended 31 May 20X1 is provided:

• Closing stock has been valued at £3,800.

• Rent and rates of £1,050 were prepaid.

• Heat and light of £260 was accrued.

• £1,500 was owed to creditors.

• Cash discounts received from suppliers in the year were £1,280.

• Depreciation is to be charged, straight line 10% on the lease and 20% fixtures and fittings. A full year's depreciation is to be charged in the year of acquisition.

Required:

(a) Determine the sales for the year.

(b) Determine the purchases for the year.

(c) Show accounts for heat and light and rent and rates, to determine the charge for the current year.

(d) Prepare a trading profit and loss account for the year ended 31 May 20X1, and a balance sheet at that date.

 Workbook Activity 8

Diane Kelly has been employed for several years supplying cleaning materials to schools, restaurants, public houses and industrial units.

She operates an incomplete system of accounting records for her business, from which the following information is available.

1	Assets and liabilities	1 June 20X0 £	31 May 20X1 £
	Warehouse fittings (NBV)	8,000	?
	Van (at cost)	–	6,500
	Stocks	10,000	16,000
	Trade debtors	16,000	19,000
	Trade creditors	15,000	20,000
	Rates prepaid	1,200	1,600
	Accruals		
	Telephone	400	500
	Heat and light	300	500

2	Bank account summary for the year	£	£
	Balance at 1 June 20X0		9,800
	Receipts		
	Debtors	79,000	
	Cash sales banked	7,700	
	Proceeds of sale of caravan	2,500	89,200
	Payments		
	Creditors	70,000	
	Purchase of van	6,500	
	Heat and light	1,800	
	Office expenses	2,600	
	Rent and rates	4,200	
	Telephone	1,200	
	Wages	9,800	
	Van expenses	1,200	
	Insurance	800	98,100
	Balance at 31 May X1		900

Notes

- The caravan was Diane's own personal property.

- All fixed assets are depreciated on the reducing balance basis, a rate of 20% is applied.

- The van was acquired on 1 June 20X0.

- During the year cash discounts of £1,100 had been allowed and £1,800 had been received.

- Diane had paid sundry office expenses by cash £420 and used £15,600 for personal reasons – both these items had been taken from the proceeds of cash sales.

- All the remaining cash had been banked.

Required:

(a) Determine the sales for the year.

(b) Determine the purchases for the year.

(c) Show accounts for rates, telephone and heat and light to determine the charge for the year.

(d) Prepare the trading, profit and loss account for the year ended 31 May 20X1 and a balance sheet at that date.

Workbook Activity 9

(a) A business marks up its goods by 60%. Sales are £200,000 for the year. What is the gross profit?

(b) A business makes a 30% margin on its sales. Opening stock is £40,000, closing stock is £10,000 and purchases are £180,000. What is the amount of sales?

 Workbook Activity 10

Data

A friend of Donald Johnson, Sheena Gordon, has been trading for just over 12 months as a dressmaker.

She has kept no accounting records at all, and she is worried that she may need professional help to sort out her financial position.

Knowing that Donald Johnson runs a successful business, Sheena Gordon approached him for advice. He recommended that you, his bookkeeper, should help Sheena Gordon.

You meet with Sheena Gordon and discuss the information that you require her to give you.

Sometime later, you receive a letter from Sheena Gordon providing you with the information that you requested, as follows:

(a) She started her business on 1 October 20X2. She opened a business bank account and paid in £5,000 of her savings.

(b) During October she bought the equipment and the stock of materials that she needed. The equipment cost £4,000 and the stock of materials cost £1,800. All of this was paid for out of the business bank account.

(c) A summary of the business bank account for the 12 months ended 30 September 20X3 showed the following:

	£		£
Capital	5,000	Equipment	4,000
Cash banked	27,000	Opening stock of materials	1,800
		Purchases of materials	18,450
		General expenses	870
		Drawings	6,200
		Balance c/d	680
	_____		_____
	32,000		32,000
	_____		_____

(d) All of the sales are on a cash basis. Some of the cash is paid into the bank account while the rest is used for cash expenses. She has no idea what the total value of her sales is for the year, but she knows that from her cash received she has spent £3,800 on materials and £490 on general expenses. She took the rest of the cash not banked for her private drawings. She also keeps a cash float of £100.

(e) The gross profit margin on all sales is 50%.

(f) She estimates that all the equipment should last for five years. You therefore agree to depreciate it using the straight line method.

(g) On 30 September 20X3, the creditors for materials amounted to £1,400.

(h) She estimates that the cost of stock of materials that she had left at the end of the year was £2,200.

Task 10.1

Calculate the total purchases for the year ended 30 September 20X3.

Task 10.2

Calculate the total cost of sales for the year ended 30 September 20X3.

Task 10.3

Calculate the sales for the year ended 30 September 20X3.

Task 10.4

Show the entries that would appear in Sheena Gordon's cash account.

Task 10.5

Calculate the total drawings made by Sheena Gordon throughout the year.

Task 10.6

Calculate the figure for net profit for the year ended 30 September 20X3.

Workbook Activity 11

Fariah is a sole trader running an IT support business and prepares accounts to 31 December 20X8. The summary of her bank account is as follows.

	£		£
Balance b/d 1 Jan 20X8	25,000	Advertising	10,000
Receipts from debtors	80,000	General expenses	8,000
		Rent	9,000
		Creditors for purchases	10,000
		Drawings	36,000
		Balance at 31 Dec 20X8	32,000
	105,000		**105,000**

Debtors at 1 January 20X8 were 20,000 and at 31 December 20X8 were 30,000.

Creditors at 1 January 20X8 were 13,000 and at 31 December 20X8 were 15,000.

All Fariah's sales are on credit. One of Fariah's debtors has been made bankrupts owing her £3,400. She wrote this debt off in November 20X8.

During December 20X8 a payment of £3,000 was made for insurance which covered the period 1 November 20X8 to 31 October 20X9. Insurance is included in general expenses.

Fariah depreciated her computers at 40% reducing balance. The WDV of the computers at 1 January 20X8 was £4,600.

Task 11.1

Calculate the capital at 1 January 20X8.

Task 11.2

Prepare the journal that Fariah would have made in November 20X8 to record the write off of the irrecoverable debt.

Journal

Account name	Dr (£)	Cr (£)
Narrative		

Task 11.3

Prepare the sales ledger control account for the year ended 31 December 20X8, showing credit sales as the balancing figure.

Sales ledger control account

	£		£

Task 11.4

Prepare the purchases ledger control account for the year ended 31 December 20X8, showing credit purchases as the balancing figure.

Purchases ledger control account

	£		£

Task 11.5

Prepare the general expenses account for the year ended 31 December 20X8.

General expenses account

	£		£

Task 11.6

Calculate the depreciation that Fariah will provide for the year ended 31 December 20X8.

Task 11.7

Prepare the journal that Fariah will make at the year end to record depreciation.

Account name	Dr (£)	Cr (£)
Narrative		

Task 11.8

Prepare a trial balance at 31 December 20X8. The trial balance should show the computers at their WDV (not cost less accumulated depreciation).

WORKBOOK ACTIVITIES
ANSWERS

WORKBOOK ACTIVITIES
ANSWERS

Workbook Activities Answers

1 Preparation of final accounts for a sole trader

Workbook Activity 5

David Pedley

Profit and loss account for the year ended 31 December 20X8

	£	£
Sales		28,400
Less: Returns		(200)
		————
		28,200
Opening stock		–
Purchases	16,100	
Less: Closing stock	(2,050)	
	————	
Cost of sales		(14,050)
		————
Gross profit		14,150
Salaries	4,162	
Rent and rates	2,130	
Insurance	174	
General expenses	1,596	
	————	
Total expenses		(8,062)
		————
Net profit		6,088
		————

Balance sheet as at 31 December 20X8

	£	£
Fixed assets		
Motor van		1,700
Current assets		
Closing stock	2,050	
Trade Debtors	5,060	
Cash at bank	2,628	
Cash in hand	50	
	9,788	
Trade creditors	(6,400)	
Net current assets		3,388
Net assets		5,088
Capital account		
Capital introduced		4,100
Profit for the year (per trading and profit and loss account)		6,088
Less: Drawings		(5,100)
Proprietors funds		5,088

Workbook Activity 6

Karen Finch

Profit and loss account for the year ended 31 March 20X8

	£	£
Sales (£17,314 + £4,256)		21,570
Purchases (£10,350 + £5,672)	16,022	
Closing stock	(4,257)	
		(11,765)
Gross profit		9,805
Assistant's salary plus bonus (£2,000 + £400)	2,400	
Electricity (£560 + £170)	730	
Rent and rates	1,100	
Postage and stationery	350	
Depreciation	1,000	
Total expenses		(5,580)
Net profit		4,225

Balance sheet at 31 March 20X8

	£	£
Fixed assets		4,000
Motor van at cost		
Depreciation		(1,000)
Net book value		3,000
Current assets		
Stocks	4,257	
Trade debtors	4,256	
Cash (W1)	6,554	
	15,067	

Current liabilities		
Trade creditors	5,672	
Accruals (400 + 170)	570	
	————	
	6,242	
	————	
Net current assets		8,825
		————
Net assets		11,825
		————
Capital		10,000
Capital introduced at 1 April 20X7		
Profit for the year	4,225	
Less Drawings	2,400	
	————	
Retained profit for the year		1,825
		————
Proprietors funds		11,825
		————

Working

	1 **Cash balance at 31 March 20X8**	£	£
	Capital introduced at 1 April 20X7		10,000
	Amounts received from customers		17,314
			————
			27,314
	Salary of assistant	2,000	
	Cash paid to suppliers	10,350	
	Purchase of motor van	4,000	
	Drawings	2,400	
	Electricity	560	
	Rent and rates	1,100	
	Postage and stationery	350	
		————	20,760
			————
	Cash balance at 31 March 20X8		6,554
			————

Workbook Activity 7

(a) Ledger accounts

Closing stock (profit and loss)

	£		£
Balance to profit and loss account	3,060	Closing stock balance sheet	3,060

Closing stock (balance sheet)

	£		£
Closing stock profit and loss account	3,060	Balance c/d	3,060
	3,060		3,060
Balance b/d	3,060		

Electricity

	£		£
Per trial balance	1,490	Profit and loss	1,175
Balance b/d (132/3)		Balance c/d (1,260 × 3/12)	315
	1,490		1,490
Balance b/d	315		

Points to note:

- As regards electricity the accrual of £44 is shown on the balance sheet as a current liability, the effect of it being to increase the charge to profit and loss for electricity.

- With rates the prepayment of £315 is shown on the balance sheet as a current asset (being included between debtors and cash), the effect of it being to reduce the charge to profit and loss for rates.

- Other items on the trial balance are dealt with by

  (i) In the case of trading and profit and loss account items, debiting the relevant accounts and crediting trading and profit and loss account (in the case of income) and debiting trading and profit and loss account and crediting the relevant accounts (in the case of expenses)

(ii)   in the case of balance sheet items being carried down at the end of the year and included on the balance sheet, being brought down as the opening balances at the beginning of the next accounting period

(b)

Elmdale

Trading and profit and loss account for the year ended

31 December 20X8

	£	£
Sales		21,417
Opening stock	2,700	
Purchases	9,856	
	12,556	
Closing stock	(3,060)	
Cost of sales		9,496
Gross profit		11,921
Rates	1,175	
Electricity	423	
Wages and salaries	3,704	
Sundry expenses	2,100	
Total expenses		7,402
Net profit		4,519

2 Partnership accounts

Workbook Activity 8

Low, High and Broad

Part (a)

PROFIT AND LOSS APPROPRIATION STATEMENT FOR THE YEAR ENDED 30 APRIL 20X1

	Total £	Low £	High £	Broad £
Salary	800	–	800	–
Interest on capital	525	200	175	150
Six months to 31 October 20X0				
Six months to 30 April 20X1	525	175	175	175
Balance (2:2:1)	4,350	1,740	1,740	870
	6,200	2,115	2,890	1,195

Part (b)

Capital accounts

	Low £	High £	Broad £		Low £	High £	Broad £
Cash	1,000	–	–	Balance b/d	8,000	7,000	6,000
Balance c/d	7,000	7,000	7,000	Cash			1,000
	8,000	7,000	7,000		8,000	7,000	7,000
				Balance b/d	7,000	7,000	7,000

Current accounts

	Low £	High £	Broad £		Low £	High £	Broad £
Drawings	1,200	800	800	Balance b/d	640	560	480
Balance c/d	1,555	2,650	875	Profit apportionment	2,115	2,890	1,195
	2,755	3,450	1,675		2,755	3,450	1,675
				Balance b/d	1,555	2,650	875

Workbook Activity 9

Capital account

	(C) £	(E) £		(C) £	(E) £
31 Dec Balance c/d	26,000	20,000	31 Dec Balance b/d	26,000	20,000
	26,000	20,000	01 Jan Balance b/d	26,000	20,000
			01 Jan Balance b/d	26,000	20,000

Current account

	(C) £	(E) £		(C) £	(E) £
31 Dec Drawings	16,250	14,750	Balance b/d	6,100	5,200
31 Dec Balance c/d	10,900	11,500	31 Dec Share of profit	21,050	21,050
	27,150	26,250		27,150	26,250
			01 Jan Balance b/d	10,900	11,500

Workbook Activity 10

Note to John Turford

When the partnership is formed the amount of capital contributed by each partner will be shown as a credit entry to a capital account for each partner.

These accounts will remain fixed and will only change if a partner introduces more capital or the partnership is dissolved. The capital account balances will be shown on the balance sheet.

The profits and drawings are accounted for through each partner's current account. The current account will simply show the balance or amount of profit retained, i.e. the effect of profit share, offset by the drawings.

As an example, let's assume that your contribution to the partnership was £40,000 and after the first year of trading profits (shared 50:50) were £48,400 in total; and your drawings during the year had been £18,750.

Your capital and current accounts would be:

Capital account

	£			£
		31 Dec	Balance b/d	40,000

Current account

		£			£
31 Dec	Drawings	18,750	31 Dec	Share of profit	24,200
31 Dec	Balance c/d	5,450			
		24,200			24,200
			1 Jan	Balance b/d	5,450

NB: Your investment in the business would now be £45,450.

There could be a situation where the drawings exceed profit and therefore the account could be overdrawn, i.e. a debit not a credit balance.

Workbook Activity 11

Capital accounts

	Kate £	Ed £	Rob £		Kate £	Ed £	Rob £
				Balance b/d	50,000	40,000	
Goodwill	14,000	14,000	7,000	Goodwill	17,500	17,500	
Balance c/d	53,500	43,500	23,000	Bank			30,000
	67,500	57,500	30,000		67,500	57,500	30,000

Workbook Activity 12

Capital accounts

	Liam £	Sam £	Fred £		Liam £	Sam £	Fred £
				Balance b/d	50,000	40,000	30,000
				Current a/c	4,000		
Goodwill		9,000	9,000	Goodwill	9,000	6,000	3,000
Bank	20,000						
Loan	43,000						
Balance c/d		37,000	24,000				
	63,000	46,000	33,000		63,000	46,000	33,000

3 Incomplete records

Workbook Activity 7

(a) **Sale for the year**

	£
Takings banked	49,560
Personal drawings	10,400
Total sales	59,960

(b) **Purchases for the year**

Purchase ledger control account

	£		£
31/5/X1 Payments	36,200	01/6/X0 Balance b/d	1,200
31/5/X1 Discounts	1,280	31/5/X1 Purchases (bal fig)	37,780
Balance c/d	1,500		
	38,980		38,980

(c)

Heat and light

	£		£
31/5/X1 Payments	1,060	01/6/X0 Balance b/d	200
31/5/X1 Balance c/d	260	31/5/X1 P&L account	1,120
	1,320		1,320
		01/6/X1 Balance b/d	260

Rent and rates

	£		£
01/6/X0 Balance b/d	950	31/5/X1 Balance c/d	1,050
31/5/X1 Payments	5,400		
		31/5/X1 P&L account	5,300
	6,350		6,350
01/6/X1 Balance b/d	1,050		

(d)

**TRADING PROFIT AND LOSS ACCOUNT OF PETER RYAN
TRADING AS 'BREW-BY'US2 FOR THE YEAR ENDED 31 MAY 20X1**

	£	£
Sales		59,960
Stock at 1 June 20X0	3,500	
Add Purchases	37,780	
	41,280	
Less Stock 31 May 20X1	3,800	
Cost of goods sold		37,480
Gross profit		22,480
Discounts received		1,280
Expenses		
Wages	3,850	
Advertising	750	
Heat and light	1,120	
Insurance	400	
Rent and rates	5,300	
Shop repairs	200	
Bank charges	320	
Depreciation		
Lease (10% × £10,000)	1,000	
Fixtures (20% × £5,000)	1,000	
Total expenses		13,940
Net profit		9,820

BALANCE SHEET AS AT 31 MAY 20X1

	Cost £	Depreciation £	NBV £
Fixed assets			
Lease	10,000	3,000	7,000
Fixtures and fittings	5,000	2,200	2,800
	15,000	5,200	9,800
Current assets			
Stock		3,800	
Pre-payments		1,050	
		4,850	
Less current liabilities			
Creditors		1,500	
Accruals		260	
Bank overdraft		1,370	
		3,130	
Net current assets			1,720
Net assets			11,520
Capital		12,100	
Add Profit for year		9,820	
		21,920	
Less Drawings		10,400	
Proprietors funds			11,520

Workbook Activity 8

(a) Sales for the year

Sales ledger control account

	£		£
01/6/X0 Balance b/d	16,000	31/5/X1 Bank	79,000
31/5/X1 Sales (bal fig)	83,100	31/5/X1 Discounts	1,100
		31/5/X1 Balance c/d	19,000
	99,100		99,100
01/6/X1 Balance b/d	19,000		

	£
Credit sales	83,100
Cash sales banked	7,700
Expenses paid by cash	420
Cash for personal use	15,600
Total sales	106,820

(b) Purchases for the year

Purchase ledger control account

	£		£
31/5/X1 Payments	70,000	01/6/X0 Balance b/d	15,000
31/5/X1 Discounts	1,800	31/5/X1 (Purchases) bal fig	76,800
31/5/X1 Balance c/d	20,000		
	91,800		91,800

(c)

Rates account

	£		£
01/6/X0 Balance b/d	1,200	31/5/X1 P&L account	3,800
31/5/X1 Payments	4,200	31/5/X1 Balance c/d	1,600
	———		———
	5,400		5,400
	———		———
01/6/X1 Balance b/d	1,600		

Telephone account

	£		£
31/5/X1 Payments	1,200	01/6/X0 Balance b/d	400
31/5/X1 Balance c/d	500	31/5/X1 P&L account	1,300
	———		———
	1,700		1,700
	———		———
		01/6/X1 Balance b/d	500

Heat and light

	£		£
31/5/X1 Payments	1,800	01/6/X0 Balance b/d	300
31/5/X1 Balance c/d	500	31/5/X1 P&L account	2,000
	———		———
	2,300		2,300
	———		———
		01/6/X1 Balance b/d	500

(d)

TRADING AND PROFIT AND LOSS ACCOUNT FOR YEAR ENDED 31 MAY 20X1

	£	£
Sales		106,820
Stock – 1/6/X0	10,000	
Add Purchases	76,800	
	86,800	
Less Stocks 31/5/X1	16,000	
Cost of sales		70,800
Gross profit		36,020
Discounts received		1,800
Expenses		
Heat and light	2,000	
Office expenses (2,600 + 420)	3,020	
Rent and rates	3,800	
Telephone	1,300	
Wages	9,800	
Vehicle expenses	1,200	
Insurance	800	
Depreciation		
Warehouse fittings	1,600	
Van	1,300	
Discounts allowed	1,100	
Total expenses		25,920
Net profit for year		11,900

BALANCE SHEET AS AT 31 MAY 20X1

	£	£
Fixed assets		
Warehouse fittings		6,400
Van		5,200
		11,600
Current assets		
Stock	16,000	
Trade debtors	19,000	
Prepayments	1,600	
Cash at bank	900	
	37,500	
Less current liabilities	20,000	
Trade creditors		
Accruals	1,000	
	21,000	
Net current assets		16,500
Net assets		28,100
Capital (W)		29,300
Add Capital introduced		2,500
Add Profit for year		11,900
		43,700
Less Drawings		15,600
Proprietors funds		28,100

Working

The opening capital can be entered as the balancing figure on the balance sheet. Alternatively it can be proved as follows:

	£
Fittings	8,000
Stocks	10,000
Debtors	16,000
Creditors	(15,000)
Prepayments	1,200
Accruals	(700)
Bank	9,800
	29,300

Workbook Activity 9

(a)

	£	%
Sales	200,000	160
Cost of sales		100
Gross profit ($\frac{60}{160} \times 200,000$)	75,000	60

	£	%
Sales = (($\frac{100}{70}$) × 210,000)	300,000	100
Cost of sales (see below)	210,000	70
Gross profit	90,000	30

	£
Cost of sales	
Opening stock	40,000
Purchases	180,000
Closing stock	(10,000)
	210,000

Workbook Activity 10

Task 10.1

Total purchases

	£
Purchase of stock bought in October	1,800
Purchases (bank)	18,450
Cash payments	3,800
Closing creditors	1,400
	25,450

Task 10.2

Cost of sales

	£
Purchases	25,450
Less closing stock	2,200
	23,250

Task 10.3

Sales for the year

If GP margin on sales is 50% then sales are $£23,250 \times \dfrac{100}{50} = £46,500$

Task 10.4

Cash account			
	£		£
Cash sales	46,500	Bank contra	27,000
		Materials	3,800
		General expenses	490
		Drawings (bal fig)	15,110
		Float balance c/d	100
	46,500		46,500

Task 10.5

	£
Cash drawings (from Task 4)	15,110
Bank	6,200
	———
	21,310
	———

Task 10.6

	£
Gross profit	23,250
	———
General expenses (870 + 490)	1,360
Depreciation	800
	———
	2,160
	———
Net profit	21,090
	———

Workbook Activity 11

Task 11.1

Capital at 1 January 20X8

	£
Bank	25,000
Trade debtors	20,000
Computers	4,600
Trade creditors	(13,000)
	———
Capital	36,600
	———

Tutorial note. Remember that capital equals net assets. You therefore have to list all the assets and liabilities at the start of the year to find the net assets and therefore the capital.

Task 11.2

Journal

Account name	Dr (£)	Cr(£)
Irrecoverable debt expense	3,400	
Sales ledger control account		3,400
Narrative	Being the irrecoverable debt	

Task 11.3

Sales ledger control account

	£		£
Balance b/d 1 Jan 20X8	20,000	Cash from debtors	80,000
		Irrecoverable debt	3,400
Credit sales (bal fig)	93,400	Balance c/d 31 Dec 20X8	30,000
	113,400		113,400

Task 11.4

Purchases ledger control account

	£		£
Paid to creditors	10,000	Balance b/d 1 Jan 20X8	13,000
Balance c/d 31 Dec 20X8	15,000	Purchases (bal fig)	12,000
	25,000		25,000

Task 11.5

General expenses account

	£		£
Cash paid	8,000	P and L a/c	5,500
		Balance c/d	2,500
	8,000		8,000

Tutorial note. The £3,000 insurance covers 10 months of the following year – a prepayment of £3,000 × 10/12 = £2,500.

Task 11.6

Depreciation for the year ended 31 December 20X8

	£
WDV at 1 January 20X8	4,600
Depreciation for the year at 40%	1,840
	2,760

Task 11.7

Journal

Account name	Dr (£)	Cr(£)
Depreciation expense	1,840	
Accumulated depreciation – computers		1,840
Narrative	Being the depreciation for the fixed assets for the year	

Task 11.8

Trial balance as at 31 December 20X8

	£	£
Capital at 1 October 20X7		36,600
Bank	32,000	
Sales		93,400
Sales ledger control a/c	30,000	
Purchases	12,000	
Purchases ledger control a/c		15,000
Advertising	10,000	
General expenses	5,500	
Prepayment – general expenses	2,500	
Rent	9,000	
Drawings	36,000	
Depreciation expense	1,840	
Irrecoverable debt expense	3,400	
Computers	2,760	
	145,000	145,000

Tutorial note. The examiner has commented that students get this sort of question wrong because they do not methodically deal with each of the points of the question and tick them off as they are dealt with. The trial balance is an excellent guide to the completeness and accuracy of your double entry (although not a complete guarantee of accuracy!). If the trial balance does not balance try and find the error but don't spend too long looking for it.

MOCK ASSESSMENT

1 Mock Assessment Questions

SECTION 1

Task 1.1

You are working on the final accounts of a business with year end 31st March 2010. Currently the business does not use a double-entry system so you are to prepare the ledger accounts for SLCA, VAT and Bank for the first time. You have the following information:

Balances	
Account	Year End 31/03/09
	£
SLCA	292,887.00
PLCA	267,900.00
VAT owed to HMRC	32,977.00
Bank Overdraft	485.00

Details for year ended 31st March 2010

Credit sales were £422,874.00 plus VAT.

Credit purchases were £303,385.00 inclusive of VAT.

Cash sales were £109,126.95 including VAT.

Receipts from Debtors were £452,080.00 (including VAT).

Payments to Creditors were £298,456.00.

A contra was processed at the value of £9,800.00.

The business purchased a motor car costing £31,000.00 plus of VAT and paid for it with a cheque.

Office Expenses amounted to £590.00 exclusive of VAT and were paid from the bank.

The VAT owed at 31/03/09 was paid to HMRC.

Wages were paid that totalled £28,820.00.

Closing balances for Debtors and Creditors were £318,422.00 and £341,221.00 respectively.

(a) **Using the figures given above, prepare the sales ledger control account for year ended 31st March 2010. Show clearly discounts as the balancing figure.**

SLCA

Date 2010	Details	Amount £	Date 2010	Details	Amount £

(b) **Using the figures above, prepare the VAT account for year ended 31st March 2010. Show clearly the carried down figure.**

VAT

Date 2010	Details	Amount £	Date 2010	Details	Amount £

(c) **Using the figures above, prepare the Bank account for year ended 31st March 2010. Show clearly the carried down figure.**

BANK

Date 2010	Details	Amount £	Date 2010	Details	Amount £

Task 1.2

This is a task about calculating missing balances.

A sales margin of 30% applies to the business.

Sales in the period amounted to £356,455.

Purchases amounted to £213,699.50.

Closing Stock amounted to £45,382.

(a) **Draw up the Trading Account clearly showing the figure for opening stock.**

Trading account	£	£

(b) **Using the information in the table below calculate the capital invested during the year. At the start of the year the balance on the capital account was £43,000.**

Assets and Liabilities at Year End 2010	£
Motor Vehicles	130,000.00
Stock	45,760.00
Debtors	97,447.00
Bank	11,978.00
Creditors	65,398.00
Loan	20,000.00
Capital	?
Profit	148,677.00
Drawings	6,890.00

(c) **Tick the boxes to show what effect this transaction will have on the balances:**

A decrease in the allowance for doubtful debts.

Account name	Debit ✓	Credit ✓	No change ✓
Allowance for doubtful debts			
SLCA			
Allowance for doubtful debts adjustment			
Sales			

(d) **Choose one Balance Sheet classification for each account.**

Account name	Fixed assets ✓	Long-term liability ✓	Current asset ✓	Current liability ✓
VAT refund				
Land				
SLCA				
Loan owed back in 11 months				

KAPLAN PUBLISHING

SECTION 2

Task 2.1

Section 2 of this exam is based on a partnership made up of three partners – Brett, Mat and Bernard. You are completing the accounts related to years ending 31st March 2010.

General Information:

Financial Year Ending 31st March 2009

- At the beginning of financial year, the profit sharing ratio was as follows:

  Brett – 40%

  Mat – 20%

  Bernard – 40%

- Bernard left the partnership on 31st December 2008. Goodwill was valued at £250,000 on this date.

- For the rest of the financial year, the profit sharing ratio for Brett and Mat was 3:1.

Trial Balance as at 31st March 2009	DR	CR
	£	£
Accruals		452
Administration Expenses	35,879	
Allowance for Doubtful Debts		1,300
Allowance for Doubtful Debts Adjustment		344
Bank		198
Capital - Brett		80,000
Capital - Mat		40,000
Cash	5,800	
Closing Stock	2,350	2,350.00
Current - Brett	1,340	
Current - Mat		4,120
Depreciation Charge	9,990	
Discounts Received		422
Disposal	4,300	
Equipment Cost	227,000	
Equipment Accumulated Depreciation		46,700
Heat, Light and Gas	6,670	
Loan		34,000
Opening Stock	3,700	
PLCA		95,630
Prepayment	2,000	
Purchases	296,789	
Purchase Returns		2,346
Rent	8,000	
Sales		475,632
Sales Returns	1,646	
SLCA	103,450	
VAT		14,620
Wages	89,200	
	798,114	798,114

KAPLAN PUBLISHING

Prepare the Profit and Loss for the Partnership for the Year Ended 31st March 2009 based on the trial balance above. All year-end adjustments have been made.

	£	£
Sales		
Cost of sales		
Gross profit		
Expenses		
Net profit		

Task 2.2

You need to prepare the appropriation account for the partnership for the year ended 31st March 2009.

Further information:

Salaries:

Brett - £8,000 per annum

Bernard - £6,000 per annum

Interest on Capital awarded at 4% per annum. Brett and Mat's capital did not change during the year. Bernard had a balance of £50,000 on his capital account from the beginning of the year until he left the partnership.

	01/04/08-31/12/08	01/01/09-31/03/09	Total
Net Profit			
Salaries:			
Interest on Capital			
Residual Profit			
Profit Share:			

Task 2.3

(a) **Complete Bernard's Capital account to deal with his retirement on 31st December 2008. It has been agreed that £10,000 will be paid straight to him and the remainder set up as a loan to the Partnership.**

Further information:

The **final balance** on Bernard's current account was £3,660 (credit)

CAPITAL - BERNARD

Date 2010	Details	Amount £	Date 2010	Details	Amount £

(b) **Complete the Goodwill Account to deal with Bernard leaving the Partnership on 1st November 2010.**

GOODWILL

Date 2010	Details	Amount £	Date 2010	Details	Amount £

Task 2.4

Financial Year Ending 31st March 2010

- Richard joined the partnership on 1st November 2009. Goodwill was valued at £200,000 on this date and Richard invested £30,000 into the partnership

- For the rest of the financial year, the profit sharing ratio was as follows:

  Brett – 13/20

  Mat – 5/20

  Richard – 2/20

Trial Balance as at 31st March 2010		
	DR	CR
	£	£
Accruals		366.00
Administration Expenses	23,245.00	
Allowance for Doubtful Debts		1,300.00
Bank		755.00
Capital - Brett		120,000.00
Capital - Mat		60,000.00
Capital - Richard		30,000.00
Cash	3,873.00	
Closing Stock	2,170.00	2,170.00
Current - Brett	1,480.00	
Current - Mat		18,070.00
Current - Richard		1,200.00
Depreciation Charge	7,100.00	
Equipment Cost	290,500.00	
Equipment Accumulated Depreciation		56,690.00
Heat, Light and Gas	7,200.00	
Loan		28,000.00
Opening Stock	2,350.00	
PLCA		52,342.00
Purchases	314,577.00	
Rent	9,000.00	
Sales		544,512.00
SLCA	157,200.00	
VAT		5,390.00
Wages	102,100.00	
	920,795.00	920,795.00

All adjustments have been made in the trial balance above for the year ended 31st March 2010 apart from the share of profits.

Profit for the year has been calculated as follows:

Brett - £57452.90

Mat - £20,277.50

Richard – 3379.60

(a)   **What are the updated current account figures for the three Partners?**

	£
Brett	
Mat	
Richard	

Workings

(b) **Prepare a Balance Sheet for the Partnership as at 31st March 2010 including the above amendment to the Current Accounts.**

	£	£	£
Fixed assets			
Current assets			
Current liabilities			
Net current assets			
Long term liabilities			
Net assets			

KAPLAN PUBLISHING

1 Mock Assessment Answers

SECTION 1

Task 1.1

(a)

SLCA

Date 2010	Details	Amount £	Date 2010	Details	Amount £
1/04/09	Bal b/d	292887.00	31/03/10	Bank	452080.00
31/03/10	Sales	496876.95		Contra	9800.00
				Discounts	9461.95
				Bal c/d	318422.00
		789763.95			789763.95

(b)

VAT

Date 2010	Details	Amount £	Date 2010	Details	Amount £
31/03/10	Purchases	45185.00	1/04/09	Bal b/d	32977.00
31/03/10	Office exps	103.25	31/03/10	Credit sales	74002.95
31/03/10	Bank	32977.00	31/03/10	Cash sales	16252.95
	Bal c/d	44967.65			
		123232.90			123232.90

(c)

BANK

Date 2010	Details	Amount £	Date 2010	Details	Amount £
31/03/10	Sales	109126.95	01/04/09	Bal b/d	485.00
31/03/10	SLCA	452080.00	31/03/10	PLCA	298456.00
			31/03/10	Motor vehicles	36425.00
			31/03/10	Office exps	693.25
				VAT	32977.00
			31/03/10	Wages	28820.00
			31/03/10		
		561206.95			561206.95

Task 1.2

(a)

Trading account	£	£	%
Sales		356,455.00	100
Opening stock	81,201.00		
Purchases	213,699.50		
Closing stock (bal fig)	(45,382.00)		
Cost of sales (356,455.00 x 70/100)		249,518.50	70
Gross profit (356,455.00 x 30/100)		106,936.50	30

(b)

	£
Opening Capital	43,000
Capital introduced	15,000
Add profit	148,677
Less drawings	6,890
Net assets	199,787

(c)

Account name	Debit ✓	Credit ✓	No change ✓
Allowance for doubtful debts	✓		
SLCA			✓
Allowance for doubtful debts adjustment		✓	
Sales			✓

(d)

Account name	Fixed assets ✓	Long-term liability ✓	Current asset ✓	Current liability ✓
VAT refund			✓	
Land	✓			
SLCA			✓	
Loan owed back in 11 months				✓

SECTION 2

Task 2.1

	£	£
Sales		473,986
Cost of sales		
Opening stock	3,700	
Purchases	294,443	
Closing stock	(2,350)	295,793
Gross profit		178,193
Sundry income		
Discounts received		422
Allowance for doubtful debt adjustment		344
Expenses		
Administration expenses	35,879	
Depreciation charge	9,990	
Disposal	4,300	
Heat, light and gas	6,670	
Rent	8,000	
Wages	89,200	153,695
Net profit		24,920

Task 2.2

	01/04/08-31/12/08	01/01/09-31/03/09	Total
Net Profit	18,690	6,230	24,920
Salaries:			
Brett	6,000	2,000	8,000
Bernard	4,500	0	4,500
Mat	0	0	0
Interest on Capital			
Brett	2,400	800	3,200
Bernard	1,500	0	1,500
Mat	1,200	400	1,600
Residual Profit	3,090	3,030	6,120
Profit Share:			
Brett	1,236.00	2,272.50	3,508.50
Bernard	1,236.00	0	1,236.00
Mat	618.00	757.50	1,375.50

Task 2.3

(a)

CAPITAL - BERNARD

Date 2010	Details	Amount £	Date 2010	Details	Amount £
31/03/10	Bank	10,000	1/04/09	Bal b/d	50,000
31/03/10	Loan	143,660	31/03/10	Current a/c	3,660
			31/03/10	Goodwill	100,000
		153,660			153,660

(b)

GOODWILL

Date 2010	Details	Amount £	Date 2010	Details	Amount £
31/03/10	Capital – Brett	100,000	31/03/10	Capital – Brett	187,500
	Capital - Mat	50,000		Capital – Mat	62,500
	Capital - Bernard	100,000			
		250,000			250,000

Task 2.4

(a)

	£
Brett (-1480 + 57452.90)	55,972.90
Mat (18,070 + 20,277.50)	38,347.50
Richard (1,200 + 3,379.60)	4,579.60

(b)

	£	£	£
Fixed assets			
Equipment	290,500	56,690	**233,810**
Current assets			
Stock		2,170	
Debtors		155,900	
Cash		3,873	
		161,943	
Current liabilities			
Creditors		52,342	
VAT		5,390	
Accruals		366	
Bank		755	
		58,853	
Net current assets			**103,090**
Long term liabilities			
Loan			28,000
Net assets			**308,900**
Capital – Brett			120,000
Capital - Mat			60,000
Capital - Richard			30,000
Current – Brett			55,973
Current – Mat			38,347
Current - Richard			4,580
			308,900

INDEX

KAPLAN PUBLISHING